GENESIS to REVELATION

ACTS

JAMES E. SARGENT

PARTICIPANT

GENESIS to REVELATION

ACTS

JAMES E. SARGENT

PARTICIPANT

GENESIS TO REVELATION SERIES: **ACTS**
PARTICIPANT

ISBN 978-1-501-84811-7

Manufactured in the United States of America

17 18 19 20 21 22 23 24 25 26—10 9 8 7 6 5 4 3 2 1

ABINGDON PRESS
Nashville

TABLE OF CONTENTS

You will be my witnesses in Jerusalem, and in all Judea and Samaria, and to the ends of the earth (1:8).

1

THE MISSION TO THE WORLD AND PENTECOST

Acts 1–2

DIMENSION ONE: WHAT DOES THE BIBLE SAY?

Answer these questions by reading Acts 1

1. To whom is this book written? (1:1)

2. For how many days did Jesus appear to the apostles? (1:3)

3. What are Jesus' instructions to the apostles? (1:4-5)

4. Who are the apostles, according to the list in Acts 1:13?

5. Who is the first preacher? (1:15)

6. How many people are numbered as believers? (1:15)

7. What are the requirements to be an apostle? (1:21-22)

8. Who is selected as the twelfth apostle? (1:26)

Answer these questions by reading Acts 2

9. When are the apostles "all together in one place"? (2:1)

10. What charge is leveled against the apostles? (2:13)

11. Which Old Testament prophet does Peter quote? (2:17-21)

12. What does Peter recall from the life of Jesus? (2:22-24)

13. How do the apostles know of the Resurrection? (2:32)

14. What is the result of Peter's preaching? (2:37)

15. To whom is the promise of forgiveness available? (2:39)

16. How many are baptized that first Pentecost? (2:41)

17. To what do believers devote themselves? (2:42)

18. How does the writer of Acts characterize the Christian community? (2:44-46)

19. How are Christians viewed by outsiders? (2:47)

DIMENSION TWO: WHAT DOES THE BIBLE MEAN?

■ **Acts 1:1-5.** Acts is not a single work. Acts is the second part of a larger work. Here the writer gathers up the tradition of the earlier work by referring to "all that Jesus began to do and to teach." Now Jesus continues the work. "After his suffering, he presented himself to [the apostles] and gave many convincing proofs that he was alive. He appeared to them over a period of forty days and spoke about the kingdom of God." The fact of Jesus' resurrection and subsequent appearances is central to the early Christian movement.

Jesus speaks of the kingdom of God and tells the apostles to await the coming of the Spirit in Jerusalem. Jesus gives a great promise to the apostles: Whereas John baptized with water, Jesus' followers will be baptized with the Holy Spirit (verses 3-5).

■ **Acts 1:6-11.** *The Ascension.* As the disciples gather they are vitally concerned with two burning issues. How soon will the Kingdom come? And to whom will the promise of the Kingdom be given? They hope for a swift coming and for national restoration.

Jesus confronts the apostles' attitude by telling them that God's timing is not for them to know. Then Jesus gives the apostles a word of encouragement—"you will receive power"—and of indefinite challenge—"you will be my witnesses."

As soon as Jesus' last words are spoken, Jesus is lifted up and he disappears in a cloud. In an unguarded moment, the apostles continue "looking intently up into the sky."

- **Acts 1:12-14.** With the promise of Jesus' return fresh in their minds, the apostles return the short distance to Jerusalem. In Jerusalem they gather in an upper room where they pray.
- **Acts 1:15-26.** The first preaching in Acts is done by the apostle Peter. As he stands, the company is noted to be of about one hundred and twenty persons. Peter's preaching is a reflection of what the earliest Christian community believes. One of the major elements of this belief must be the fulfillment of Scripture, for Peter cites passages from Psalms 69 and 109 in his sermon.

In his sermon Peter contends that the events that brought about the arrest, conviction, and crucifixion of Jesus were not merely mistakes of history that got out of control and that eventually overwhelmed an innocent man. To the contrary, Peter sees the events as part of something that had been in the mind of God and that is contained in the Scriptures: "Brothers and sisters, the Scripture had to be fulfilled" (1:16).

Peter gives an explanation for what happened to Judas after his treachery. The tradition in Matthew tells of Judas hanging himself (Matthew 27:3-10). In this tradition Peter concludes that Judas bought a small farm. An accident of some kind occurred there that killed Judas. The field then became known by the Hebrew name *Akeldama*.

Anyone who would be an apostle had to meet certain requirements. (1) He would have been with Jesus during his entire ministry from the baptism to the Ascension. This would mean that (2) he would be an eyewitness to the resurrected Jesus. (3) An apostle had to be chosen by God as well. Two men meet these requirements, Joseph called Barsabbas and Matthias.

The apostles pray. Characteristic to the entire movement is the prayer that is shared by not only the apostles but by all Christians. In this instance the community prays for the one whom God has chosen to fill the vacancy. The central event of choosing rests with God.

The first chapter of Acts concludes with the selection of a twelfth apostle. Once again there are twelve who will be the major eyewitnesses to Jesus' resurrection. They already have been promised the Spirit.

■ **Acts 2:1-13.** Jews for centuries had gathered for a celebration of the harvest. This celebration took place on the fiftieth day following the morning of the Passover sabbath. On this day the first fruits of the grain harvest were offered in the temple as a thank-offering to the Lord. Acts 2 opens with the new Christian element of the Jewish tradition gathered for the Feast of Pentecost (fiftieth day). The first of a great harvest of converts were gathered in, giving promise of a remarkable number yet to come.

Suddenly, without any warning, something like the rush of a violent wind swept over them. Every corner of the house felt the in-rushing. As to precisely what occurred, of course, we can do no more than wish to know more. The images of rushing wind and tongues of fire were readily available images to a Jewish tradition. The tongues of fire resting atop each of the gathered persons would have reminded them of the element of divinity. Something of extraordinary dimension and power happened that day. The writer concludes that "all of them were filled with the [promised] Holy Spirit."

At the same moment Jews from many nations, who therefore spoke different languages, heard the commotion and outburst. These devout folks were bewildered, for never before in their Holy City had they been able to understand more than a word or two picked up in the marketplace (verses 6-8). Many wonder exactly what this phenomenon means. Others can only scoff at the event by charging the apostles with drunkenness. The gospel becomes life and power with the followers of Jesus. Jesus as an external presence becomes indwelling Spirit.

■ **Acts 2:14-36.** *Peter's Pentecost sermon.* To the charge of drunkenness, Peter contends that at only nine o'clock in the morning these men are not drunk. More to the point, an ancient Scripture has been fulfilled, Joel 2:28-32. Here Peter gives the Christian interpretation of this Scripture, interpreting the ancient Scripture in light of Jesus of Nazareth. God had worked through Jesus' signs and wonders. This same Jesus, Peter says, was delivered up not by some terrible mistake. Rather, the intention of God was being worked out, just as the Scriptures said it would be. Jesus was delivered up and crucified (verses 23-24). But Jesus did not remain dead; God raised Jesus from the grave. For the Christian, the single fact of the Resurrection is the central fact in the faith.

The sermon continues with another reference to the Scriptures. Here Psalm 16:8-11 is cited. Especially in verse 10 is the Resurrection seen.

> Because you will not abandon me to the
> realm of the dead,
> you will not let your holy one see decay.
> (Acts 2:27)

Clearly it was not David's body that did not know corruption. This psalm is seen as a promise for the Davidic Messiah.

Peter continues with his interpretation of Jesus' life in light of the ancient Psalms. In verse 30, Peter refers to Psalm 132:11, which tells of the ancient Jewish hope of a descendant of David on the throne. God's faithfulness through the establishment of such a descendant fulfills Jewish hopes. The fulfillment, Peter says, is not through the triumphant political military messiah for which the majority of Jews had hoped. Instead, this hoped-for Messiah is the crucified and resurrected One.

Jesus is also now the exalted One at the right hand of God (verse 33).

Once more, Peter returns to his interpretation of the Scriptures. Psalm 110:1 is cited, thus giving scriptural authority to the Ascension and exaltation of the crucified and resurrected Jesus.

■ **Acts 2:37-43.** The sermon has an immediate impact. The listeners are "cut to the heart" and can only ask what they can do. Peter's response captures the basic rhythm of Christian tradition: "Repent and be baptized." The gift of the Holy Spirit is clearly the result of repentance and forgiveness.

The promise of the forgiveness of sins and the blessing of the Holy Spirit is for all. Throughout the Book of Acts we see the struggle for a widespread, universal gospel. The previously small sect within Judaism gives evidence of becoming a phenomenally growing movement. As a result of Peter's preaching, about three thousand are baptized.

Once baptized, the converts devote themselves to the disciplines of early Christianity. Teaching or instruction by the apostles is central, as is the gathering together. The special fellowship centered around Jesus' forgiveness and presence with and within the Christian community is called *koinonia*. The *koinonia* shares a special life. The sharing of meals generally and the sharing of the Lord's Supper especially is part of the fellowship.

■ **Acts 2:44-47.** Through the exemplary living, preaching, and wondrous works of the Christians, many others are awe-struck. Luke then describes the *koinonia*. All those who believe show unity not merely in belief but in their living. All things are held in common. Goods, perhaps parcels of land, are sold in order to raise sufficient funds to help all in the community who are in need. This is a special quality of caring and sharing that emerges from the unique work of the Holy Spirit.

The chapter ends with the Lord adding regularly to the movement. A significant note is that once again the writer and presumably the Christian community assert that it is the Lord who adds to the number. It is the Lord who works through the common life, exemplary living, and wondrous work of Christians that others may be saved.

DIMENSION THREE: WHAT DOES THE BIBLE MEAN TO ME?

Pentecost and the Coming of the Spirit

The meaning of Pentecost has been variously interpreted by Christians ever since the event itself. What do you think best captures the significance of the event?

1. The apostles are overwhelmed by a mysterious power giving them the ability of ecstatic speaking.
2. The coming of the Spirit is the birthday of the church.
3. The coming of the Spirit inaugurated the long hoped-for new age.

Why do you think so? In what way would you suggest that with the presence of the Holy Spirit we live in a new age? How many Christians of our day experience a personal Pentecost?

The Christian and the Future

The word *eschatology* refers to the end time. Do you suppose the majority of people you know anticipate the inevitability of God's grace and goodness? Or do people expect the inevitability of evil? How would people act if they anticipated the triumph of God? What would behavior be if people anticipated evil?

The Old Testament and the Christian

A question that often challenges Christians is how to use the Old Testament. The problem is not a new one; it has its origins as early as the first generation of Christians. As you read the various Old Testament quotations in Peter's sermon (Psalms 69:26; 109:8; Joel 2:28-32; Psalms 16:8-11; 132:11; 16:10; 110:1), what occurs to you? How do you see today's Christian using the Old Testament? As a means by which to recover our Jewish roots? As a means by which to predict the coming of Jesus? As proof of who Jesus was and what he was to do? How do you see the writer of Acts using the Old Testament?

*After they prayed . . . they were all filled with the Holy Spirit
and spoke the word of God boldly (4:31).*

THE SIGNS AND WONDERS OF THE APOSTLES

Acts 3–5

DIMENSION ONE: WHAT DOES THE BIBLE SAY?

Answer these questions by reading Acts 3

1. Who goes to the temple to pray? (3:1)

2. In whose name is the man who was lame from birth healed? (3:6)

3. Peter declares that neither personal power nor piety healed the lame man. Whom does Peter claim healed the man? (3:13, 16)

4. What must the man have in order to be healed? (3:16)

5. What does Peter ask of the people at the conclusion of his preaching? (3:19, 26)

Answer these questions by reading Acts 4

6. Which group of Jewish leaders is disturbed by Peter's preaching? (4:1-2)

7. Why are the leaders disturbed? (4:2)

8. What are the leaders' names? (4:6)

9. What is the appearance of Peter and John? (4:13)

10. What do the authorities decide to tell the apostles? (4:18)

11. What is the apostles' response to the charge to remain silent? (4:19-20)

12. What occurs in the place where the apostles and their friends pray? (4:31)

13. Who sells a field in order to share with the apostles? (4:36-37)

Answer these questions by reading Acts 5

14. Which two people sell a field and keep some of the proceeds for themselves? (5:1-2)

15. What happens to the husband when Peter challenges him? (5:5)

16. What happens to the wife when she is confronted about the same matter? (5:10)

17. Which Jewish group responds negatively against the apostles? (5:17)

18. Who is the Pharisee in the Sanhedrin who speaks regarding the threat of the apostles? (5:34)

19. What is Gamaliel's counsel? (5:38-39)

DIMENSION TWO:
WHAT DOES THE BIBLE MEAN?

■ **Acts 3:1-10.** The remarkable power of the Spirit now works through Peter and John. A man "over forty years old" (4:22) who had been lame since birth is miraculously healed at the temple gate. The man begs as he had for years. But on this day the two Christian men, Peter and John, offer him more than money could buy. The effect is quite predictable: The man begins "walking and jumping, and praising God." The crowds are thoroughly amazed.

■ **Acts 3:11-26.** As the healed man grasps Peter and John, a large crowd rushes to see the miracle. Peter uses the opportunity for preaching. The sermon contains many of the elements of the *kerygma* (the proclamation that Jesus is the Christ and that people are saved by faith in him) that are found in all the sermons in Acts, and indeed, all the early Christian proclamations. First of all, the power of healing does not come because of personal piety, nor is it within the apostles themselves. The power is from God. This God is the one who revealed himself in Jesus. Both the name of Jesus and the faith of the lame man are responsible for the healing (verses 12-16).

Peter begins his sermon by being the bridge from a former to a current reality. He joins himself to them, calling them "fellow Israelites" and invokes the name of their revered patriarchs, Abraham, Isaac, and Jacob, who had "glorified [God's] servant Jesus." He then testifies to the history of rejection by his countrymen of this glorified son by handing him over to the religious authorities. They "disowned him," the one sent and approved by God.

After further indicting his fellow Israelites, he shifts his approach, giving them an out. "Now. . . I know that you acted in ignorance. . . . Repent, then, and turn to God." He invites and welcomes them to join him in the new fellowship of believers in "the Holy and Righteous One."

Within Peter's sermon, in all likelihood a composite of many elements of early preaching, are the central truths to which the *kerygma* gives witness.

■ **Acts 4:1-22.** The miraculous healing not only stirred awe within the crowd, it provoked one specific segment of the Jews—the Sadducees. Sadducees, who were wealthy, educated men, supported a conservative interpretation of the Law. One of their doctrinal differences with the more moderate Pharisees was over the notion of the resurrection from the dead.

Quite a number of Sadducean officials gather: Annas the high priest, Caiaphas who is in fact the reigning high priest, John, and Alexander, as well as others of the ruling aristocracy. This body presents itself up against two common men. The apostles, surrounded by antagonists, are asked to explain themselves: "By what power or what name did you do this?"

This confrontation once again gives Peter the opportunity for preaching. Luke describes Peter as "filled with the Holy Spirit," thus giving him immense power of courage and of expression. Peter gains the upper hand by calling the proceedings a trial. The reason for the trial is not by any means clear. Is the healing itself cause for interrogation? Or is the manner or authority by which the healing took place the real issue? Peter assumes the latter. He says in effect, "Jesus Christ of Nazareth is the name by which the healing has been accomplished. This man, whom you see before you healed, was healed by the same Jesus whom you rejected." Peter then continues, almost tripping over the words, until finally in an outburst of enthusiasm and confidence he declares there is no salvation in anyone else other than Jesus (verse 12).

Taken aback by such boldness and confidence in an apparently uneducated man, the Sadducees wonder. Then they recognize the apostles as some of those who had been with Jesus of Nazareth. Evidently up to this time the link had not been made. But now the Sadducees saw not only the apostles but the accomplished fact of a healed man right in front of them. What could be done? After the apostles are dismissed a debate springs up. The miracle cannot be denied. The power and attendant authority of the Christians must be restricted; it has already spread far enough. In an attempt to restrict the gospel, the apostles are then charged to keep silent about Jesus.

However, Peter will not knuckle under to the authorities. The Sadducees are welcome to make up their own minds, but the apostles must witness to what they have seen. The scene concludes with the crowds praising God because of what has been done through the Christians.

■ **Acts 4:23-31.** After their release the apostles go directly to their fellow Christians to share the news of what has happened. Under threat of further violence, the Christian fellowship prays. The prayer follows roughly the prayer in Isaiah 37:16-20. Trust in their sovereign Lord, Maker and Sustainer of the universe, will sustain them. Sufferings and tribulations are not a surprise. They are part of God's plan, even to the extent that the trials and sufferings of Jesus are no fluke. Even now God will sustain (verses 29-30).

■ **Acts 4:32–5:11.** The next two stories show conflicting conditions in the church. The first is that of communal care and integrity. All members of the community gave up their personal claims to property. This does not necessarily mean that private property ceased to exist. Certainly, individuals owned property. However, when need arose, as inevitably it would, the church depended on the spirit of sacrifice and self-denial of the believers. This fact shows that from the outset caring for those who are in need has been important to the Christian community. Distribution is handled by the leaders, presumably the apostles at whose feet the goods and money are placed.

Barnabas appears here as an ideal individual (verses 36-37). Later he will appear in Acts as a major figure in the life of Saul and in the missionary work (Acts 9:27; 11:22-30; 12:25–13:12; 13:42-50; and other places). Does the episode represent a general trend? Or is it here because of its uniqueness? The answer to this question is still debated. Clearly, from what follows, not all members of the church are of equal integrity.

Two believers, Ananias and his wife Sapphira, sell a piece of property. However, in sharp contrast to Barnabas, these two conspire to keep part of the money for themselves. Nothing suggests that keeping part of the money is improper, or even that they were required to give any of the proceeds. The sin is in their attempt to lie to the apostles and the church as well as to the Holy Spirit. Peter knows immediately that a conspiracy has been hatched. The charge is quickly elevated from a sin against human beings to a sin against God, at which time Ananias dies immediately (5:5). Do not try to explain this incident in psychological terms. To do so is to read a twenty-first-century mindset back into a first-century document. Much more to the point, Luke is presenting an illustration of God's immediate judgment. The shock of the severity and extent of the judgment stuns onlookers.

Three hours later the same judgment comes to Sapphira, the other conspirator. Caught in her lie, Sapphira is told that footsteps can be heard. The men who are approaching are those who have just buried Ananias. She then dies and is buried (verses 7-10).

Why are the two stories inserted here? The flow of the narrative could easily have moved directly from 4:31 to 5:12. Especially the story of Ananias and Sapphira gives evidence that the struggling Christian church has internal stress as well as external stress. Such a description of internal and external stress prevents an overly idyllic picture of how the church spread and grew. Modern readers can be thankful for such vivid glimpses and insights into church life.

■ **Acts 5:12-16.** Luke now brings the signs and wonders of the apostles to the forefront. Evidently the apostles did not heed the Sadducees' admonition to stop healing and preaching. Still, enough threat was present that not all who saw what the apostles did joined them; some still kept a relatively safe distance (verse 13).

■ **Acts 5:17-42.** As in the earlier episode the high priest and other Sadducees rise up against the apostles. The apostles are arrested and jailed. But this time an angel intervenes to release them. Once released the apostles make their way to the temple where at daybreak they preach. Their primary concern seems to be the continued defiance of given orders. But the officials must be careful as the Christians are greatly admired by the crowd and have a large following. Any heavy-handed persecution may yield only a riot.

This defiance and offense enrages the authorities. Except for the intervention of the well-respected Gamaliel, Christians would have had their first martyrs. Gamaliel's argument is a short and powerful one. He says in effect, "Others have presented themselves as would-be saviors. And each of them is remembered as a failure. But we must be aware that if this important movement is of human origin it will fail of its own accord. If it is legitimately from God then we may be fighting God." The white-hot anger of the Sadducees is cooled by the argument. Rather than death, the apostles endure a flogging. One outstanding feature at the conclusion of the matter is that the punished Christians rejoice since they had been able to suffer for the name of Jesus (2 Corinthians 1:5).

DIMENSION THREE: WHAT DOES THE BIBLE MEAN TO ME?

Acts 4:5-21—*The Action of the Holy Spirit*

The dramatic confrontation between the Sadducean officials and the apostles raises the issue of how the Holy Spirit works. What gave the apostles sufficient courage to resist the threat? Clearly Luke presents the presence of the Spirit as their encouragement.

What situations confront Christians today with the dilemma of either silence or witness in the face of threat? Do any issues demand a Christian response and then threaten anyone who dares make an assertion?

Acts 3:10; 4:21; 5:34-39—*Relationship Between Christians and Jews*

Among the most difficult dilemmas Christians have faced over the centuries is the relationship that exists between Christian and Jew. What different perceptions do you have about this relationship? Are any of them anti-Jewish? inflammatory?

What are the dangers of anti-Semitic feelings when reading the New Testament? How might a rereading of Gamaliel's intervention affect these perceptions? This entire study will attempt to illustrate the tragic element in salvation rather than condemn anyone or any group of people. The tragedy is that some will purposely reject the offer of salvation; others will seek to restrict the scope of that offer. In either event, the tragic side of human experience is all too clearly apparent.

Acts 4:3-4; 5:17-26—A Gospel That Cannot Be Contained

Throughout Acts, Luke portrays many attempts to contain the gospel of Jesus Christ. In Acts 3–5, the attempt is largely an external one. The apostles are jailed, flogged, and told not to preach or teach Jesus as the Christ. What modern attempts to contain the gospel can you think of?

What are the implications of the inability to contain the gospel for people under totalitarian regimes? Can the gospel be contained today by those who control the media, police, and military forces?

So the word of God spread. The number of disciples in Jerusalem increased rapidly (6:7).

STEPHEN AND PHILIP

Acts 6–8

DIMENSION ONE: WHAT DOES THE BIBLE SAY?

Answer these questions by reading Acts 6

1. Who are the people who are upset about suspected prejudice? (6:1)

2. Who are chosen as servers? (6:5)

3. How are the servers authorized for their work? (6:6)

4. With whom does Stephen come into conflict? (6:9)

5. What is the charge against Stephen? (6:14)

6. How is Stephen's appearance described? (6:15)

Answer these questions by reading Acts 7

7. Who begins the interrogation of Stephen? (7:1)

8. How does Stephen describe his listeners? (7:51)

9. How do Stephen's listeners react to his charge, and what do they do to him? (7:54-58)

10. Who is a witness to the death of Stephen? (7:58)

11. What are Stephen's final words? (7:59-60)

Answer these questions by reading Acts 8

12. Following Stephen's death what happens to the church? (8:1)

13. All Christians are scattered except for whom? (8:1)

14. Who is named as one of the worst persecutors of the church? (8:3)

15. Who goes to Samaria to preach? (8:5)

16. Who is the sorcerer with whom Philip comes into conflict? (8:9)

17. How does Simon seek to obtain the Holy Spirit's presence and power? (8:18-19)

18. On his way back to Jerusalem, where is Philip told to go? (8:26)

19. To whom does Philip interpret the Scripture? (8:27-35)

20. What else does Philip do for the eunuch? (8:38)

DIMENSION TWO:
WHAT DOES THE BIBLE MEAN?

In these chapters Christianity comes under increasingly strong resistance and attack. Persecution breaks out, driving Christians out of the confines of Jerusalem into other parts of the Holy Land and beyond. God uses these scattered people as the means by which to expand Christianity across geographical, national, and racial barriers.

■ **Acts 6:1-6.** The Christian movement has already attracted Greek-speaking Jews, Hellenists who have come from all over to live in Jerusalem. Not surprisingly conflict develops between the groups of people over distribution of aid to the Hellenists. The Twelve decide that a division of responsibilities is required. The congregation is given the authority to select seven men of excellent reputation to be servers, thus freeing time for the Twelve for prayer and preaching.

■ **Acts 6:8-15.** Up until now Christianity has enjoyed the respect of many and only a relative disdain from the Sadducees. The Hellenistic Jews confront Stephen about his wonders and great works that appeal to many people.

Presumably his interpretation of Scripture and preaching causes offense as well. The best arguments the Jews raise are not sufficient to silence Stephen as he has been empowered by the Spirit. Since argument does not work, the offended Jews conspire to bring charges of blasphemy against Stephen.

■ **Acts 7:1-53.** By far the longest speech in the Book of Acts, Stephen's speech retells the history of Israel. What distinguishes this speech is the manner in which Stephen reinterprets history. By subtle alteration and specific emphases Stephen indicts Israel for its refusal to hear the word of God as it is spoken through chosen men sent by God.

The first indictment is that God first spoke to the patriarch Abraham. The fact that Abraham received no land, except a burial plot he purchased (Genesis 23), is altered. Even without land and as a sojourner, indeed threatened with slavery, Abraham is offered the covenant of circumcision.

The Joseph story is told next. Still God remains with Joseph, the outcast brother, even in Egypt. Jacob and his sons are "brought back to Shechem" and are buried in a foreign land—the despised Samaria.

Moses' story provides Stephen with the first strong indictment of Israel and, by implication, the present audience for their refusal to hear the words of a man sent from God (verses 25, 35). In the Exodus account of Moses' flight from Egypt he flees because the Egyptian overlords have found out about the killing. In this speech Stephen's reinterpretation shows Moses fleeing because of his own people (verses 27-29).

The same man whom the Hebrews had rejected now leads them through the Red Sea and through the desert for forty years. In the desert, even as Moses received the "living words" (the Ten Commandments), the Israelites refused to hear him. The forceful phrase "pushed him aside" (NRSV, verse 39; "rejected" in the NIV) adds to their burden of refusal. Rather than worship God, Israel sought idols and other works of their hands.

In addition to the refusal to hear the words of God through Moses, the Israelites under David and Solomon chose to build a temple rather than retain the Tabernacle as God's dwelling place. God does not dwell in a specific place (verse 48).

Using the stinging language of the prophet Jeremiah (9:25-26), Stephen condemns Israel as a stiff-necked people who refuse to listen to the Holy Spirit. Stephen then makes the charge that his whole speech has led to: You have betrayed and killed the Righteous One—the Messiah—Jesus.

■ **Acts 7:54–8:1a.** Stephen's audience is enraged at his charges and attack him. Stripped of his garments, Stephen is chased into the streets and is stoned to death. Luke places Saul as an observer to the death: the clothes of the "witnesses" are placed at Saul's feet. Reminiscent of Jesus' last words, Stephen asks to be received and then asks forgiveness for the persecutors (7:59-60).

■ **Acts 8:1b-3.** Following the death of Stephen a storm of persecution rages against the Christians in Jerusalem. Christians are driven from Jerusalem into the surrounding regions.

Samaria is the hilly country to the north, formerly a part of the Northern Kingdom of Israel. The native population had been deported during the Assyrian onslaught centuries earlier. The Assyrians repopulated the region with people from throughout the empire. Thus the Samaritans had always been considered half-Jews at best. Now the Christian movement will make its first major step toward a universal gospel by spreading into this formerly despised area.

■ **Acts 8:4-8.** During the time between Stephen's death and Paul's missions to the Gentiles, Philip and other anonymous disciples carry the word of God into the world.

Luke's purpose, therefore, is not primarily to illustrate the geographical expansion of Christianity. The barriers through which the gospel has to go are national, racial, and cultural.

Under the leading of the Spirit the flight from danger in Jerusalem is transformed into missionary work. The work begins with Philip. Philip's preaching is confirmed by the miracles he performs as well.

Living in the same region is Simon, a sorcerer. Impressed by the power of Philip's work, Simon too is baptized without a firm grasp as to just what it is that Philip preaches. Simon, no doubt representative of many people, completely misses the meaning of the Holy Spirit. For Simon a price can be found and paid for any power. He makes an offer. Peter, stunned by the crass materialism of the would-be wonderworker, rejects the offer outright (verse 20).

■ **Acts 8:26-40.** Philip's encounter with the Ethiopian eunuch again gives an exciting drama illustrating the expansion of Christianity. This episode is directed by the Spirit. The Spirit's guidance is essential in order to validate the mission. The Christian missionary movement is more than the result of jealous, self-directed people.

The application of the suffering servant image to Jesus is the first specific use of Isaiah 53 in the New Testament. Philip interprets the life and meaning of Jesus through the Scriptures (verses 32-35).

The baptism scene has few details—the body of water cannot be identified, and only a few ancient authorities include a baptismal confession. Verse 37 is therefore omitted in the New International Version and the New Revised Standard Version.

DIMENSION THREE: WHAT DOES THE BIBLE MEAN TO ME?

Acts 7:1-53—The Problem of History and National Pride

Stephen's speech on one level is a retelling of Israel's history. On another level, however, Stephen reinterprets Israel's history by criticizing the ancients (and by implication the current listeners) for their refusal to follow the guidance of God's appointed ones (Moses, the prophets, and Jesus). We are able to sit at a comfortable distance agreeing with the indictments and not feeling any of the white-hot rage that seethed in Stephen's listeners.

Begin this discussion by imagining why the Sadducees and others got so angry. How would we respond if we heard someone indict us for the way we ignored the plight of Native Americans? How would we respond if we were criticized for not listening to Martin Luther King, Jr.? What might our response be?

Acts 8:6-8—Miracles of Healing

Among the most troubling aspects of biblical study is the meaning of the miracles. In Acts the miracles illustrate the power of God. The miracles lead toward repentance and in some instances baptism.

What is the danger of seeing the miracles without the relationship to repentance and baptism? Are miracles today related to how people should live? Are there any legitimate miracles in our time?

Acts 7:1-53—Preaching as an Event

Think about what preaching does. Is preaching merely an exhortation to get people to repent and become Christian? Does preaching tell people what to do? Is the preacher responsible for telling an excellent story fifty-two times a year?

Preaching as a radical event implies that when the preacher preaches, the will of God somehow teaches the hearts and souls of the hearer. What would happen if congregations perceived preaching as a radical event? What constitutes a preaching event?

*I now realize how true it is that God does not show favoritism
but accepts from every nation the one who fears him
and does what is right (10:34-35).*

THE CONVERSION OF PAUL AND CORNELIUS

Acts 9–10

DIMENSION ONE: WHAT DOES THE BIBLE SAY?

Answer these questions by reading Acts 9

1. Who continues his threats against the disciples of Jesus? (9:1)

2. To which city does Saul travel? (9:2)

3. What happens on the road to Damascus? (9:3-6)

4. Who is instructed to find Saul? (9:10-12)

5. What is God's response to Ananias's objection? (9:15)

6. What does Saul do when he hears of the conspiracy against him? (9:23-25)

7. Peter speaks the name of Jesus Christ in order to heal which man in Lydda? (9:34)

8. Whom does Peter revive at Joppa? (9:36-41)

Answer these questions by reading Acts 10

9. Who is the centurion of the Italian Regiment in Caesarea? (10:1)

10. Who is lodging with Simon the tanner in Joppa? (10:5-6)

11. What does Peter see in his vision? (10:10-12)

12. What is God's answer to Peter's hesitancy? (10:15)

13. As Peter wonders about the meaning of the vision, who arrives? (10:17)

14. What happens when Cornelius and Peter finally meet? (10:25-29)

15. What is Peter's reason for associating with non-Jews? (10:34-35)

16. In whose name are the Gentiles baptized? (10:48)

DIMENSION TWO: WHAT DOES THE BIBLE MEAN?

In this lesson you will study the conversion and initial ministry of Saul/Paul as well as the first tentative Christian contacts with the Gentiles. Keep in mind that Luke's account has thus far shown Christianity well founded within the Jewish traditional structures of worship and the temple. The first expansion, as we have seen, was to the hated Samaritans and to "God-fearers." The end of Acts 8 leaves the reader in surprise. What would become of the persecuted church?

■ **Acts 9:1-9.** Saul, introduced earlier at the stoning of Stephen (8:1), is the major character persecuting the Christians. Authorized by the chief priest in Jerusalem, Saul intends to inflict further damage on the beleaguered people of the Way. As he proceeds, an event of remarkable proportions takes place.

This story is repeated with only minor changes two more times in Acts (22:4-16; 26:9-18). Three repetitions indicate the importance of the conversion. Here a light from heaven flashes about Saul, causing him to fall to the ground. A voice asks, "Saul, Saul, why do you persecute me?" Saul learns that it is Jesus who asks him this question. Saul is then instructed to get up and continue to Damascus where he will receive instructions as to what he is to do. The point is, of course, that when Saul persecutes the Christian movement he persecutes Jesus. For three days Saul remains blind because of the bright light.

■ **Acts 9:10-19a.** Ananias, one of the Christians in Damascus whom Saul had planned to arrest, receives disturbing instructions. He is to seek Saul whom the Lord has already notified. Ananias, fully aware of the feared persecutor, protests. He describes what Saul has done to Christians in Jerusalem. Protest, however, is not the final word. Ananias learns that God has much in mind for Saul. Saul is to be "my chosen instrument to proclaim my name to the Gentiles and their kings and to the people of Israel." Note the order in which the missionary fields are listed. Also note that the missionary work will involve suffering (verse 16).

Ananias proceeds directly to the house in which Saul had been praying. Using the familiar Christian greeting *brother*, he first explains the reason for this remarkable event. Saul, who had been blind for three days and quite without knowledge of precisely how his affliction would be resolved, hears from Ananias that the same Jesus who appeared to Saul as a blinding flash of light has sent help. Immediately Saul's sight is restored. Following his healing Saul receives Christian baptism in the fellowship of those who only days before he was intent on harassing.

■ **Acts 9:19b-25.** Saul then seeks synagogues in which he, much to the amazement of all, proclaims the Christian interpretation of the Scriptures and Jesus as the Christ. Saul's preaching of the Christian doctrine offends many Jews, who plot to kill him.

■ **Acts 9:26-31.** Returning to Jerusalem Saul meets the same distrust that he had seen in Damascus Christians. They do not dare trust him. Perhaps he is only setting them up by trying to infiltrate their small community. Barnabas serves to bear the brunt of leadership for the moment (verse 27). These two men (Barnabas and Saul) will develop a strong relationship.

■ **Acts 9:32-43.** At Lydda, northwest of Jerusalem, Peter meets a Christian named Aeneas, who had been paralyzed for at least eight years. Speaking the name of Jesus Christ,

Peter heals him. This miracle, as in earlier instances, prompts both wonder and faith in the land throughout the region. In Joppa (present-day Jaffa) Peter is called to the bedside of Tabitha (in Greek, Dorcas), a woman known for her good works, who has died of illness. Peter kneels over her and tells her to rise. Incredibly she is revived. This second healing brings faith and wonder to the region around Joppa.

Thus Luke's stories get Peter to the city of Joppa in preparation for the next major development in the growth of the church, the first conversion of a Gentile. Keep in mind that up until this point, Christian expansion has been within Judaism itself or those associated with Judaism.

■ **Acts 10:1-8.** At Caesarea lives a centurion named Cornelius who serves in the army, the Italian Regiment. He is described as "devout and God-fearing; he gave generously to those in need and prayed to God regularly" (verse 2). God approaches Cornelius through the vision of an angel. Though terrified, Cornelius is told to send messengers to Joppa to get Peter.

■ **Acts 10:9-16.** As the messengers near Joppa, Peter is approached by God through a vision. As a meal is being prepared, Peter in his hunger has a vision of a large container with all sorts of animals in it. His first impulse on being told to kill and eat is to balk. Some of the animals are those forbidden to Jews (Leviticus 11). Three times God tells Peter to eat and "do not call anything impure that God has made clean." Evidently Peter does not grasp the significance of the vision.

■ **Acts 10:17-23a.** While Peter is still puzzled, Cornelius's messengers arrive. The Spirit has to tell him to answer the door! When Peter finally receives the visitors, they tell him the strange events that have taken place recently.

Luke tells the story with many references to the divine direction that planned it all. The reason for this is to show that the initial movement to the Gentiles was not merely the decision of a few strong-willed men. Indeed, the

Christians themselves resisted the directive, or they did not comprehend what God intended. None of the participants has a complete grasp of the events nor of their significance. Throughout Acts, Luke's major theological concerns are centered on the action of the Spirit and the reason for the Gentile mission. Chapter 10 gives strong evidence of this concern.

■ **Acts 10:23b-33.** Peter, along with some other Christians from Joppa, goes with the messengers to Caesarea. Cornelius anticipates their return and has gathered his family and friends for the occasion. The meeting of the two men creates an awareness for the apostle (as Cornelius does not yet understand) of precisely what these events mean. Breaking out of centuries of tradition Peter now has the insight necessary to understand the vision. God does not intend further barriers to be put between people.

■ **Acts 10:34-43.** The vision that had thoroughly puzzled Peter was clearly not about clean and unclean food animals; the vision had to do with people and how God looks on them. Peter's insight then becomes the first moment of mission to the Gentiles. God does not restrict the possibility of saving faith to any single people (the Jews). God intends for people from every nation who fear him and do what is right to be acceptable.

Once again the promise and hope of the universal gospel is expressed (verse 43). All who believe will receive forgiveness of sins. *Universal* in this sense does not imply that all people regardless of their response to Christ know the forgiveness of sins. The hope of the gospel is for a universal claim with no restrictions with respect to access due to race, national origin, or culture.

■ **Acts 10:44-48.** As Peter preaches, the Holy Spirit comes on all those who hear the preaching. The Spirit gives them the ability of "speaking in tongues." Many readers confuse this event with the event of Pentecost during which time people spoke in different languages. Both demonstrations give evidence of the Spirit's presence. However, we must be careful not to put both events into a single category. The Holy Spirit is free to be expressed in various forms.

Luke's purpose has been to show God's initiative for the gospel to be spread to the Gentiles. The issue is not yet settled.

DIMENSION THREE: WHAT DOES THE BIBLE MEAN TO ME?

Acts 9:1-9—Wrong Actions for Good Reasons

Religious zeal has both negative and positive results. Saul had studied his Scriptures (our Old Testament), which tells many stories of the people of God inflicting injury on enemies—all in the name of this God. He was prepared to kill Christian converts, also in the name of God. Yet Paul's zeal is what enabled him to endure incredible hardships to be one of the earliest and greatest missionaries and theologians of the Christian era.

In a world climate in which religious zeal (including Christian religion) may lead to violence or oppression, how are we to gauge when actions "cross the line"? What authority defines when zeal is appropriate? On the other end of the scale, how do we justify a lack of zeal (or a penchant for safety and comfort) as a reason to keep from effectively acting upon our faith?

Acts 9:10-19a, 26-29; 10:9-16, 47—God's Imperative and Our Reluctance

Luke's story of the early church includes a picture of the resistance to the instruction of the Holy Spirit. Luke uses individual events to represent larger movements. Therefore, we can conclude that in the early years of the church significant resistance against the mission to the Gentiles emerged. The leading of the Holy Spirit was clearly not easy to discern.

How do we know the direction in which God is leading us as individuals? As a church? How do you determine the leading of the Holy Spirit? What direction(s) might your life or the life of your church take if only the leading of the Holy Spirit were heeded?

Acts 9:1-9—Conversions

Many books have been written on conversion. For the purposes of convenience, I want to suggest the following process of conversion:

1. A moral issue is at stake.
2. Past perceptions are not sufficient. In a person's life a gap exists between the moral issue (whatever it is) and the previous thinking or attitude about it.
3. The person is aware of the need for a different behavior or attitude.
4. The person has the courage to act on the new awareness or attitude.

Can you recall the time when you became aware of a moral issue to which you had to make some sort of response? What was the new attitude you knew you had to adopt? How did you summon sufficient courage to act on the new attitude or awareness?

But the word of God continued to spread and flourish (12:24).

THE MISSION TO THE GENTILES

Acts 11–12

DIMENSION ONE: WHAT DOES THE BIBLE SAY?

Answer these questions by reading Acts 11

1. In which city are the apostles and the believers gathered? (11:2)

2. What is the response to Peter's explanation of his vision and encounter with the Gentiles? (11:18)

3. To which cities and regions had Christians fled as a result of persecution? (11:19)

4. When the church in Jerusalem hears of the preaching to Gentiles, whom do they send to Antioch? (11:22)

5. How is Barnabas described? (11:24)

6. Where else does Barnabas go? (11:25)

7. What name is given for the first time to followers of Jesus in Antioch? (11:26)

8. Which prophet predicts severe famine? (11:28)

9. What is the Christian response to the famine? (11:29)

10. Who is entrusted with taking the collection to Jerusalem? (11:30)

Answer these questions by reading Acts 12

11. Who begins a new wave of persecution against the Christian movement? (12:1)

12. Which of the Twelve is killed during this persecution? (12:2)

13. Who is then arrested? (12:3)

14. How is Peter rescued? (12:7-10)

15. What is the congregation's reaction to Peter's release? (12:12-16)

16. What does Herod do when he learns of the escape? (12:19)

17. How is Herod punished for his persecution and blasphemy? (12:20-23)

18. What is Luke's conclusion as to the effect of this persecution? (12:24)

19. Who travels with Barnabas and Saul? (12:25)

20. What are some turning points in Acts? Fill in the blanks.

Luke presents many turning points in Acts. The gospel is first preached within the ranks of "both _____ and _____" (2:11). Then the gospel spreads to the formerly despised _____ (8:5) represented by _____ (8:9). The next expansion takes place with _____ (10:1-2). In Acts 11 and 12, the Christian movement finally begins to reach out to the _____ (11:1).

DIMENSION TWO:
WHAT DOES THE BIBLE MEAN?

Acts 11:1-18. Peter's work with Gentiles requires explanation since the Christian movement to this point is still a group within Judaism. Resistance to the Gentiles comes from the "circumcised believers" (verse 2). From Luke's description, we cannot determine whether the conservative party was already formed into a group or whether they were in the process of forming around this central issue. The charge seems to have centered on eating with "uncircumcised men" rather than on the rite of circumcision itself.

Animals of all sorts filled the "large sheet" (verses 5-9). At this point Peter does not explain the meaning of the animals and foods. For the purposes of keeping the conservatives in suspense, Luke does not allow Peter a premature disclosure of the vision's meaning.

Slight variations appear in Peter's report in the following verses. We must keep in mind that Luke's purpose is to show the reader just how significant this incidence of missionary contact with a Gentile is. Repetition serves to emphasize, and variation keeps interest sharp.

Luke uses Peter's insight (verse 17) not only to show how objection by the conservative element is stopped for the moment. By using this literary technique Luke captures the reader in the unfolding drama.

Peter's defense seems to have silenced the opponents. This silence, however, gives a false sense of resolution to the problem. The entire issue of mission to the Gentiles will be sharply debated at a later time (Acts 15).

■ **Acts 11:19-26.** The story of 8:1 is now resumed. The Jerusalem church has survived the persecution. Other Christians have scattered. Luke names three regions: Phoenicia, Cyprus, and Antioch in Syria. Luke's concern is not to detail each stream of expansion but rather to show how the Christian movement was not and could not be crushed.

In a subtle and forthright manner, Luke gives unmistakable clues as to the divisions and disagreements that existed in the Christian church from its beginning. While reading this book we simply cannot disregard the authentic conflicts that challenged the church's life, nor can we gloss over the substantive issues raised.

Despite the conflict, the church continues its growth (verse 21). News of this expansion (perhaps even the spreading to Hellenists) gets back to the home church in Jerusalem. Barnabas, a man of high stature in the congregation and whose name would have been well-known to the Christians, is sent to Antioch. The reason for the mission is not stated directly. Probably he was responsible for officially endorsing the missionary work being done with Gentiles. Since Barnabas stands in such high repute, the Antioch congregation is encouraged by his preaching to remain faithful and steadfast.

In Antioch the Christian movement is first acknowledged as distinct from Judaism and not merely a sect or separate party. In all likelihood the term *Christian* was first used as a derogatory term.

■ **Acts 11:27-30.** A prophet from Jerusalem, Agabus, predicts a famine "over the entire Roman world." The Christian disciples take an offering in order to aid the Judean Christians in their plight. The collection is to be taken by Barnabas and Saul to the elders in Jerusalem.

■ **Acts 12:1-5.** Another wave of persecution breaks over the Christian movement. The grandson of Herod the Great, Herod Agrippa I, attempts to eradicate Christianity by killing, among others, one of the Twelve. James's death is the only one of the Twelve mentioned by Luke.

To this point Luke has presented Christianity in conflict only with Sadducees (who do not hold the doctrine of resurrection). The current surge of persecution pleases not just Sadducees but all Jews (verse 3). Herod Agrippa takes the widespread support of his evil as mandate to arrest even more Christians. Thus Peter is arrested also, during the season of Passover. Arrested by four squads of soldiers, Peter will be executed on the morrow.

■ **Acts 12:6-11.** As a means by which to underscore the miraculous rescue of Peter about to take place, Luke paints a detailed description of how desperate Peter's condition really is. Sleeping between two soldiers, bound with chains and guarded by sentries outside the door, Peter has absolutely no chance of survival. Luke presses the miraculous release even further by picturing Peter fast asleep as the rescue occurs. This dramatic rescue has a hint of comedy, as the angel first pokes Peter to awaken him, and then even tells Peter how to dress!

As with the earlier vision, Peter seems almost painfully unaware of exactly what is happening to him, as it seems like just a dream. Through this picture Luke shows that the work Peter carries out is by no means Peter's own design. The missionary enterprise is the result of the Holy Spirit's leading.

■ **Acts 12:12-17.** What follows is the second hint of comedy. Peter seeks out the home where his friends have been praying for him. Standing outside, knocking hard enough to be heard yet anxious lest his noise should arouse soldiers, Peter waits. Rhoda, the maid who went to the door, recognizes his voice. But Peter cannot be there because no one escapes from the Roman soldiers. She loses her wits and leaves Peter standing outside with the door closed in his face. Rhoda runs to tell the Christians that their prayers have been answered. They tell her she is crazy! At best it can only be his guardian angel.

This guardian angel has the last laugh. Peter's persistent knocking finally distracts them from scoffing at the maid. Peter is still outside, only now with astonished friends babbling to him.

Clearly Luke uses his best literary talent, and through humor tells the absolutely inconceivable magnitude of God's work.

■ **Acts 12:18-19.** Over against the strength of God the opponents of the Christian movement are very weak indeed. In this sequel to the miracle Luke almost casually relates the frustration of Herod and the execution of the guards. Luke shows no remorse over the deaths, either of the soldiers or Herod (verse 23). The message is clear.

Anyone standing in the way of God's intention will suffer the consequences.

■ **Acts 12:20-25.** Herod seeks vengeance. The first readers of Acts would have seen immediately the stark contrast between the courageous Christian stance, which refuses to knuckle under the official threat, and the crowd mindlessly repeating the demanded response. God sustains the courageous few through the Spirit. Indeed, even with drastic oppression, the word of God grew (verse 24).

This section concludes with Barnabas and Saul returning from (or to, see footnote in NIV) Jerusalem, taking with them John Mark. Luke closes the scene with the introduction of a new character as well as the continued strong connection between the Christian churches in Jerusalem and in Antioch.

DIMENSION THREE: WHAT DOES THE BIBLE MEAN TO ME?

A careful reading of Acts 11 and 12 reveals resistance to the gospel from two directions. The first resistance took the form of oppression and persecution from outsiders. What the Christians had to endure is painfully clear through the stories of Stephen's death and Peter's imprisonment. Does similar resistance occur today? What is some of the external opposition to the gospel of Christ today?

The second form of resistance to the gospel's thrust is neither easily discerned nor readily examined. This resistance is the sort to which Luke alludes in the account of the conservative circumcision party in the Jerusalem church (11:2-3). Nothing evil was intended by this group. They merely wanted to protect and preserve what had been sacred to them and what, to them, was part and parcel of being the authentic people of God.

Luke's attitude, however, is unmistakable, they are resisting the direction of the Spirit. The gospel's movement is toward greater inclusiveness. In what ways do you see the church resisting the inclusiveness of the gospel today? What do you feel are your own resistances?

Acts 11:27-30—Human Need and the Opportunity for Ministry

In every church I have attended as a member or served as a minister the amount of money that goes to the larger church is always debated. Luke's short account of the plight of the Jerusalem church gives evidence that, first, no single church exists independently of other Christian congregations. Second, whenever or wherever need occurs we find an opportunity for shared ministry.

In what manner has your church chosen to bear a part of the burden for the relief effort in your community and in the world?

Acts 12:6-11—Divine Initiative and Human Responsibility

The dramatic rescue of Peter poses a particular problem. On the one hand is the action of God, which occurs without any human participation at all. The account shows clearly that Peter is without an active role. Some might suggest that this then becomes a model for faithful living. That is, wait for the Holy Spirit to act.

However, faithful living also includes daring and risk-taking. Luke's implications regarding this ever-expanding mission of the Christian movement are quite clear. Yes, the disciples and apostles are directed by the Spirit. But by the same token, they must act courageously on the basis of what they know at the moment. Therefore, authentic faithful living will by and large be in that ambiguous realm of tension between the absolute dependence on the Spirit and the trust in risk-taking.

Where do you see your congregation living with the tension and ambiguity of authentic faithfulness? Where do you feel the tension between the leading of the Spirit and the need to act without absolute certainty?

Set apart for me Barnabas and Saul
for the work to which I have called them (13:2).

THE FIRST MISSIONARY JOURNEY

Acts 13–14

DIMENSION ONE: WHAT DOES THE BIBLE SAY?

Answer these questions by reading Acts 13

1. Who are the prophets and teachers in Antioch? (13:1)

2. Which two men are designated by the Holy Spirit for a special work? (13:2-3)

3. Who directs the missionaries on their journey? (13:4)

4. Who summons Barnabas and Saul in order to hear the word of God? (13:7)

5. What happens to the false prophet Elymas (Bar-Jesus) when he tries to keep Sergius Paulus from the faith? (13:11)

6. Which missionary leaves Paul and the others in the middle of the journey? (13:13)

7. Where and to whom does Paul address his proclamation? (13:14-16, 26)

8. What is the reaction to Paul's preaching? (13:42-44)

9. Why do Paul and Barnabas speak to the Gentiles? (13:45-46)

10. How do Paul and Barnabas react to the persecution stirred up against them? (13:50-52)

Answer these questions by reading Acts 14

11. When the missionaries preach in the Iconium synagogue, what is the result? (14:2-5)

12. What is the reaction to Paul's healing of the man in Lystra who is lame? (14:11-13)

13. What happens when Jews from Antioch and Iconium arrive? (14:19)

14. After Paul recovers from the stoning, what does he do? (14:20-22)

15. Through what must Christians pass in order to enter the kingdom of God? (14:22)

16. What do Paul and Barnabas tell the church? (14:27)

17. Complete the following sketch of the first missionary journey:

From Antioch the missionaries go to _____ (13:4) from which they sail to _____ (13:4). Upon arriving at _____ (13:5) they preach to Jews in synagogues. Traveling west through Cyprus the missionaries arrive in _____ (13:6). After the encounter with the magician Elymas, Paul and his company go to _____ in Pamphylia (13:13). After John (Mark) departs, the balance of the company proceed to _____ (13:14). Persecution drives the missionaries out of Antioch to _____ (13:51). When the Christian missionaries learn of an impending persecution, they flee to _____ and _____, cities of Lycaonia (14:6). After completing the mission the men return to _____, _____, and _____ (14:21). The rest of the journey goes through _____ and _____ (14:24). After preaching in _____ (14:25) they go to _____ (14:25). From here they sail back to _____ (14:26).

DIMENSION TWO: WHAT DOES THE BIBLE MEAN?

In this lesson you will study the first of three missionary journeys undertaken by the apostle Paul. Luke's account of the mission to the Gentiles sets the stage for the central event in Acts, the Council in Jerusalem (Acts 15).

■ **Acts 13:1-12.** Luke starts by describing the church in Antioch. Barnabas and Saul (Paul) are singled out by the Holy Spirit for "the work to which I have called them." The others join in by the laying on of hands and send them off.

From Antioch in Syria the missionaries travel to Seleucia from which they sail to the island of Cyprus. Salamis, on the eastern coast of Cyprus, is the first stop. Two notes should be made. First, the missionaries sought out Jews in the synagogue. Second, Luke subtly includes John (verse 5). With scarcely any mention of results the missionaries move across the entire island to the western harbor of Paphos where the major event of the Cyprus mission takes place.

Christianity had to contend with the allure of mystery religions and magic throughout its early years. Luke uses this incident of the sorcerer Elymas to illustrate the conflict. The proconsul Sergius Paulus wants to hear the preaching, but the magician says no. For the first time Paul confronts resistance and emerges victorious. Not only does Paul thereby become a victorious figure, the Christian faith is shown to be far superior to the magic of magicians.

■ **Acts 13:13-16.** After the successful mission in Paphos Paul and his company sail for Asia Minor, landing at Perga, in Pamphylia. Here John leaves the mission for Jerusalem.

From Perga the company proceeds to Antioch in Pisidia. Note that the missionaries seek to speak to Jews in the context of synagogue worship. On the sabbath the preachers attend the sabbath service. Following the usual opening service, the visitors are invited to speak.

Paul begins by addressing the Jews ("Fellow Israelites") and the God-fearers ("you Gentiles who worship God").

■ **Acts 13:17-41.** A three-part sermon takes shape. First, God has prepared the people for God's revelation through their history: the long slavery in Egypt; the desert wandering; subduing the land of Canaan with its seven hostile tribes; rule by a series of judges; the monarchy, beginning with Saul and culminating in David, to whom so many promises were made. The preaching of the early church, the *kerygma*, used Scripture as a means of proof. Throughout this sermon, Paul refers to various Old Testament passages.

The familiar promise to the Davidic line is then repeated. From the Christian perspective, of course, the promise comes to focus in the person of Jesus.

The coming of Jesus was foretold by John the Baptist, who preached a baptism of repentance. But John was not the one who was to come. Thus preparation by God has been completed.

Second, God has sent his Son to the world. The sermon now focuses on the gospel message of Jesus, still addressed "Fellow children of Abraham and . . . God-fearing Gentiles" (verse 26).

The *kerygma* is once again preached. The death of Jesus was scripturally foretold. Paul says that Jesus' death came as a result of ignorance on the part of Jewish leaders. Jesus' innocence is established clearly.

Third, God raised Jesus in order to offer forgiveness to us. The gospel message turns on the resurrection of Jesus from the dead.

Indeed, Jesus is raised from the grave, the promise of God fulfilled (Psalms 2:7; 16:10; Isaiah 55:3), and to this the apostles are eyewitnesses.

■ **Acts 13:42-52.** The following sabbath Paul again addresses the congregation. In this sermon he explains the reason why he first approached the Jews. Then, since the Jews have excluded themselves from the gospel, he goes to the Gentiles, citing Isaiah 49:6 for his scriptural authority. The Gentile mission begins to reap immense results immediately. The Christian gospel begins to spread throughout the region.

By way of reinforcing the picture of the missionaries choosing to extend their journey and spread the gospel, Luke characterizes them as filled with joy and the Holy Spirit. Note Luke's subtle manner of indicating the leading by the Spirit rather than the demand of circumstance forcing missionaries onward.

■ **Acts 14:1-7.** Iconium, a Roman city in Galatia, is the next major city to which the Christian gospel is taken. Once again the missioners seek out Jews in the synagogue.

Resistance begins almost immediately. Because of the resistance or due to the number of converts, the missionaries stay in Iconium for a long time. Not surprisingly, the city is divided between those sympathetic to the plight of the threatened Jews and those thrilled by the new proclamation of God's work through Christ.

Yet another plot develops against the missionaries (verse 5). When the missionaries hear of the plot, they leave. In Acts persecution never achieves its goal of eliminating the Christian movement. Indeed, persecution in every instance works to spread the movement further and further throughout the Roman Empire.

■ **Acts 14:8-18.** Luke tells a story not only of another miraculous healing but of the larger incidence of contact between the Christian faith and the other religions and superstitions of the time. In Lystra, Paul heals a man who is lame. Once again the extent of the man's affliction is exaggerated in order to emphasize the immense power of God.

After the man is healed the crowd is amazed and starts talking in their native language, referring to Barnabas and Paul as Zeus and Hermes, the names of their local gods. As Paul and Barnabas watch the reaction of the crowd they are appalled. When the priest of Zeus prepares a sacrifice for the missionaries (not to make a sacrifice *of them*!), Paul refuses to be worshiped. Beginning with elements of their religion (a god providing rain, crops, food, and joy), he reframes it to mean the Christian understanding of God, using nature as his reference rather than Scripture.

■ **Acts 14:19-23.** Even while they are surrounded by worshipers of Roman gods, the missionaries are haunted by persistent Jews who have come from Antioch and Iconium. Paul is stoned, dragged out of the city, and left for dead.

Either Paul's wounds were not that severe or he recovered quickly, for the next day he and his fellow missionaries continue their journey to Derbe. Luke is indicating that Christians should anticipate suffering and hardship because of their beliefs.

The return trip passes without any further mention of missionary activity. Luke's purpose has been fulfilled. The missionary enterprise of the Christian movement has extended through to the pagan elements of the world.

DIMENSION THREE: WHAT DOES THE BIBLE MEAN TO ME?

Acts 13:13-14; 14:8-18—*The God of the Commonplace*

Readers of Acts may wonder how the missionaries lived their lives on ordinary days. Luke spends little time describing the mundane issues of financing boat trips, outfitting journeys across mountain ranges, or making a living during the week. The spectacular work of miracle-working and avoiding or withstanding persecution occupies center stage. But what of the commonplace in the lives of apostles, missionaries, and other Christians?

The first readers of Luke's Gospel and Acts were churches struggling to maintain the foothold they had been able to establish in the sometimes hostile environment of the Roman Empire. We may be tempted when reading Acts to see the miraculous and spectacular as the normal Christian witness. Such a reading, however, leaves the majority of us out of the good news. One scholar has suggested that the work of the apostles took up much of the week. Therefore, they could only preach when they themselves, like their hosts and audiences, had the time free from work on the sabbath. Discuss the importance of sharing one's Christian witness in whatever our vocational setting happens to be. Could it be that more converts have been gained by the intimate witness of individual Christians sharing in the commonplace events of life than have been gained by means of the more spectacular and miraculous?

Acts 14:21-25—Discipleship of a Sterner Sort

During the return journey through cities in which Christian congregations had only recently been formed, the missionaries encouraged Christians to hold fast to the faith. The only way we enter the Kingdom is through trial, tribulation, and death. This sort of discipleship is a stern sort indeed. What shall we do with such a demanding faith?

Have you heard Christian discipleship described in these sorts of terms? Is this the kind of faith that people want to hear preached? What would your church say to such a demanding presentation of the invitation to discipleship?

God, who knows the heart, showed that he accepted them by giving the Holy Spirit to them, just as he did to us (15:8).

7

THE JERUSALEM COUNCIL TO THE GENTILES

Acts 15:1–16:5

DIMENSION ONE: WHAT DOES THE BIBLE SAY?

Answer these questions by reading Acts 15

1. What are the men from Judea teaching that Paul and Barnabas object to? (15:1-2)

2. To which city do Paul and Barnabas, along with some others, then proceed? (15:2)

3. What is the initial response to the returning missionaries? (15:4)

4. What is the objection raised to the mission to the Gentiles? (15:5)

5. Summarize Peter's argument. (15:7-11)

6. What is the assembly's response? (15:12)

7. Who speaks after Peter? (15:12)

8. Summarize James's argument. (15:13-21)

9. When debate in the Jerusalem Council concludes, which men are sent to Antioch? (15:22)

10. Summarize the letter sent to Antioch. (15:23-29)

11. What is the response to the compromise? (15:31)

12. Which disciples remain preaching and teaching in Antioch? (15:35)

13. Describe the conflict that arises between Paul and Barnabas. (15:37-40)

14. Where do Paul and Silas go? (15:41)

Answer these questions by reading Acts 16:1-5

15. Which disciple does Paul meet in Lystra? (16:1)

16. What is done to Timothy before the journey continues? Why? (16:3)

17. What is reported to the cities along the journey? (16:4)

18. How does Luke summarize the beginning of the second missionary journey? (16:5)

DIMENSION TWO: WHAT DOES THE BIBLE MEAN?

This lesson centers on the Council at Jerusalem, the center of the Book of Acts physically and in its importance for the expansion and mission of the Christian church. We will, therefore, spend a good deal of time studying the issues at stake and the decisions of the assembly.

■ **Acts 15:1-5.** The Council itself is called by a minority of conservative Christians who question the Gentile mission. Initially the issue is circumcision for males. This rite has always been a central element of Jewish identity.

After quite a conflict the decision is made to resolve the issue in Jerusalem. As Paul, Barnabas, and unnamed others proceed to Jerusalem, they pass through Phoenicia and Samaria where they visit Christian congregations, reporting the successes of the Gentile mission. Luke thus notes the existence of Christian congregations without an explanation as to how they were formed. The reaction among these congregations to the Gentile mission is one of great joy. The Jerusalem congregation also welcomes the missionaries.

The believers who make up the "party of the Pharisees" restate their belief about circumcision. The tradition of Mosaic law must be maintained in order for Gentiles to be truly Christian. Luke's account implies the conservative element is a minority. But the minority voice must be heard. The decision will be made on the basis of all points of view rather than the mere silencing of a vocal dissident few.

- **Acts 15:6-11.** Serious and heated debate follows the statement of the issue. With the sound of debate and murmuring of the malcontents in the background, Peter stands to address the assembly. The Gentile mission, he says, is no fluke nor is it the design of a few of us. The mission is the choice of God, which has been expressed through Peter's preaching.

Peter restates the insight gained through his vision (Acts 10:15, 28) that God is neither prejudiced for nor against any nation or culture. God has cleansed the hearts of Gentiles by faith.

Against the intention of God stands the current demand for observance of ritual and tradition insisted on by the former Pharisees. The demand is even more than the former Jews themselves had been able to observe completely (15:10).

With a remarkable graciousness, Peter's affirmation includes the grace of God first for Gentiles and then for Jewish Christians. All will be saved through the grace of the Lord Jesus.

- **Acts 15:12-21.** The impact of Peter's speech is immediate. The assembly is silenced because of the powerful insight and logic of his witness. Presumably Paul and Barnabas take advantage of the moment's silence to give their witness to the work of the Spirit through their missionary journey.

James then assumes leadership of the assembly (verse 13). While he does not say exactly what Peter had already said, he in effect underscores the insight and implication of Peter's words. James alters Peter's initial statement only slightly. God had visited the Gentiles to take from them a people for his name. No mention is made as to the means by which the people are to be chosen. And no reference is made to Peter's preaching.

James then cites scriptural evidence for the validity of the mission from the prophet Amos (9:11-12). The true interpretation of this prophecy is not in the restoration of the Davidic throne but rather in the Jesus event. The interpretation centers on the Resurrection. Of course, the Gentiles will then seek the Lord.

Though James did not speak exactly as had Peter, his insight and conclusion are just as powerful. The church ought not interfere with the intention of God. Certain restrictions, however, should be observed by Gentile Christians. The restrictions that James suggests have nothing to do with the issue that had prompted the council (verse 20). The focus is now on what actions are necessary for Jewish Christians and Gentile Christians to follow so they may share meals together. Thus the real problem is not one of ritual or tradition. The real issue has to do with relationships. What does each group have to do to get along, to share meals with the other? The restrictions are therefore not imposed, rather they are an attempt at compromise. The restrictions are: abstinence from unchastity, from food that has been a part of a sacrifice, from blood, and from anything that has been strangled.

■ **Acts 15:22-29.** Men of great standing in the church will take the decision to various Gentile churches. Paul and Barnabas will go to Antioch with Judas, called Barsabbas, and Silas. The decision will be written in a letter (verses 23-29).

The Apostolic Decree is issued by the Jerusalem assembly. It begins with the standard formula of greeting. The entire conflict is attributed to a small, unauthorized group of people who had opposed the Gentile mission. No mention is made as to the specific issue that had been raised. But the community itself did not hold to the minority objection. Men who had risked their lives would give the good news that Gentiles are included in the Christian church without reservation. Both the direction of the Holy Spirit and the best wisdom of the church have gone into the decision that being part of the church does not require Jewishness by the Gentiles (verse 28). Certain observances, however, are necessary so that the two cultures can share meals together. The assembly's primary concern is for the continued relationship of two formerly alien cultures.

■ **Acts 15:30-35.** The church at Antioch receives the decision joyfully. Judas and Silas, both identified as prophets, remain in Antioch preaching and exhorting the Christian fellowship. They remain in Antioch for an indefinite amount of time after which they are sent back to Jerusalem.

The entire episode concludes with Paul and Barnabas continuing their work of preaching and teaching among the Christians in Antioch.

■ **Acts 15:36–16:5.** This section serves as a transition between the Jerusalem Council and the Christian missionary movement. Paul initiates the second journey, with a view to revisit the churches that had been established earlier.

Paul and Barnabas have a major falling out. Indeed, they cease working together as a result of the conflict. Luke's account centers around John Mark's desertion on the first missionary trip. Paul's own witness makes the conflict much more substantive in nature (Galatians 2:1-13). In any event, the two men who had worked side by side for much of the first journey now separate. Paul begins working with Silas while Barnabas begins his work with John Mark. Paul and Silas continue through Syria and Cilicia on what is now the second missionary journey.

In Lystra they meet Timothy, a Christian disciple born of a Jewish mother and a Greek father. The young man is well thought of in the area. Incredibly, Paul has the young man circumcised—and this right after the conflict so recently resolved in the Jerusalem Council. For many readers, this is a glaring inconsistency. But for Paul, no convention or tradition would be either binding or heinous.

His concern seems to be that in no manner does he want to offend the people to whom he is extending the Christian gospel. Therefore, Timothy is circumcised.

Luke concludes with a summary verse. The Spirit obviously blesses the work as churches grow in numerical strength and in the faith (16:5).

DIMENSION THREE: WHAT DOES THE BIBLE MEAN TO ME?

Acts 15:1-21—The Jerusalem Council or The Peril of Prejudice

We run grave risk if we consider the only problem facing the early church was that of circumcision. The problem ran far deeper than that of observing Jewish tradition. The problem is much more that of prejudice between cultures and with different groups. The problem, therefore, is one shared by each of us in our churches.

What element of society would you find hard to accept into your church membership? Perhaps you prefer those who are economically up to the par of the congregation. Prejudice and discrimination are the curse that the Jerusalem Council had to contend with.

Others in our Christian churches refuse to extend to women full participation in the life of the church. What are your thoughts about ordination of women? Are the insights of Peter and James appropriate for these issues?

Racial and culture prejudice continues to blight our congregational life. What is your church's attitude toward including persons from other races or cultures in its fellowship?

Can we work toward more inclusiveness and universality with our gospel? Do you agree that discrimination both cripples the church and defies the will of God?

Acts 15:36-41—Ruptured Relationships

The separation of Paul and Barnabas confronts us with the reality of differences of opinion and principle. What are the reasons for their separation? Do you agree with Luke's lack of concern over the rupture? Would you suggest that sometimes a relationship has to be ended due to a disagreement over principle? Have you ever had to end a relationship due to disagreement over an ideal or value?

*"What must I do to be saved?" . . . "Believe in
the Lord Jesus, and you will be saved" (16:30-31).*

THE SECOND MISSIONARY JOURNEY

Acts 16:6–18:22

DIMENSION ONE: WHAT DOES THE BIBLE SAY?

Answer these questions by reading Acts 16:6-40

1. Describe Paul's vision at Troas. (16:8-10)

2. Where do the missionaries go to preach in Philippi? (16:13)

3. What happens to Paul and Silas as a result of healing a young slave girl? (16:19-24)

4. Why won't Paul simply leave the jail after his release? (16:37-39)

Answer these questions by reading Acts 17

5. Where does Paul go to preach on reaching Thessalonica? (17:1-2)

6. What is the result of Paul's preaching? (17:4-5)

7. What prompts Paul's speech in Athens? (17:16)

8. Paul's speech centers on the saying "to an unknown god." How does Paul suggest this god is a knowable god? (17:24-31)

Answer these questions by reading Acts 18:1-22

9. What trade does Paul practice with Aquila and Priscilla? (18:3)

10. What is the assurance Paul receives in his vision? (18:9-10)

11. What is the attitude of the Roman official toward the Jewish protests against Paul? (18:14-16)

12. When Paul preaches in Ephesus where does he go to preach? (18:19)

13. Complete the following outline of Paul's second missionary journey.

From Syrian Antioch, Paul goes through _____ and _____ strengthening churches (15:41). He travels west to _____ and _____ where he meets Timothy (16:1). Passing through the regions of _____ and _____ (16:6), he arrives at the place opposite Mysia where he is forbidden to pass over into Bithynia. Following his vision at _____ (16:8-9), he seeks to go on to _____ (16:10).

Sailing from Troas Paul proceeds through _____ (16:11) and _____ (16:11) to the city of _____ (16:12). There he meets _____ (16:14). In this city Paul performs an exorcism on the slave girl who had a spirit. After the miraculous release from jail, Paul and Silas proceed through _____ and _____ (17:1) to the major city of _____ (17:1). After being hounded out of Thessalonica, the missionaries move on to _____ (17:10). There they are received kindly. Silas and Timothy remain here when Paul sails for _____ (17:14-15).

Following the success in Athens, Paul travels on to the isthmus city of _____ (18:1). Here he meets _____ and _____ (18:2). From this city the journey quickly concludes as Paul leaves for _____ by way of _____ where he cuts his hair (18:18). Passing through _____ (18:19), he proceeds to _____ (18:22) and then to the home church in _____ (18:22).

DIMENSION TWO: WHAT DOES THE BIBLE MEAN?

In this lesson you will study the second missionary journey of Paul. For sheer breathtaking drama the second journey has all the elements one could ask for: success in preaching, conversions, an exorcism, persecution, imprisonment and miraculous release, extensive travel, intrigue, contact with other religious culture, and throughout the entire journey more direction and inspiration by the Holy Spirit.

■ **Acts 16:6-10.** Twice in succession the Holy Spirit or Spirit of Jesus (the terms are used interchangeably) intervenes to prevent a planned missionary direction. The Spirit directs the movement of the missionaries away from Asia and toward Europe. However, the emphasis of these chapters is not solely on the manner in which the gospel arrives in Europe. The emphasis is still on the dramatic encounter of Christianity with other cultures and authorities.

■ **Acts 16:11-15.** Favorable winds allow for a direct passage to Philippi, the leading city though not the capital of the Roman province of Macedonia. Paul always seeks first the Jewish synagogue. In Philippi there seems to be no synagogue, so the missionaries go to the place of prayer where they meet some women.

Lydia, a merchant who sells purple goods to wealthy people, becomes a Christian and a patron of the new Christian movement. Her home will be the center of the work in Philippi (16:40).

■ **Acts 16:16-22.** Luke's first readers, as well as those who witness the next event, would have had no difficulty whatsoever with the disturbing presence of a spirit in the slave girl. Luke shows through this incident the overwhelming authority of Christianity over pagan religious superstitions and customs. Paul performs an exorcism in the name of Jesus.

Paul finds himself the target of attack by the girl's owners. Since Paul rescued the young girl from demon possession, she has now lost her economic value to her owners. The owners, however, cannot indict Paul for the exorcism since exorcism is not a punishable offense. Instead, the charge is that of sedition and disturbing the peace.

■ **Acts 16:23-34.** Without so much as a hearing before a judge, Paul and Silas are summarily beaten and thrown into jail. The scene is now set for another miracle by the Spirit. An earthquake, miraculously opening doors, and released prisoners fill the scene. Nothing, it seems, can keep God's intention or God's people encased in stone.

Against the darkness shines the jailer's desperate question regarding his own salvation (verses 27-30). Paul's answer, "Believe in the Lord Jesus," is heeded by the desperate man. Regardless of what his superiors might say or do the jailer becomes a Christian and plays the gracious host to his benefactors (verses 33-34).

Acts 16:35-40. On the following morning the authorities, without regard for the earthquake, decide that Paul and Silas are to be released. Paul then reveals his Roman citizenship. No authority dare abuse a citizen's rights, and Paul demands a public apology and restitution. Incredibly his demands are met, at least in part.

A quick visit with the Christian congregation in Lydia's house ends the missionaries' stay in Philippi (verse 40).

■ **Acts 17:1-9.** The mission moves on to Thessalonica, the capital of the province. There Paul seeks Jews in the synagogue. Remember that Paul never forsakes his people. Luke presents Paul as a man with his soul fairly torn by the tragic inability of Jews to accept the truth of Jesus as Messiah.

Luke shows two different groups and their response to Christian preaching (verse 4). Some listeners are converted, others become antagonistic. Among those attracted to the movement are influential women and men. Luke thus shows that the Christian movement is considerably more than a small movement attracting only rabble and "ne'er do wells."

Some Jews, threatened by the success of the Christians, launch a resistance (verse 5). The riotous mob cannot find the Christian preachers so it unleashes its wrath on Jason, a follower of the gospel.

■ **Acts 17:10-15.** Paul and Silas are secreted off to Berea. Once again persecution does not quench the Christian movement; persecution expands the ministry of the gospel. After a successful time in Berea, malcontents from Thessalonica arrive to stir up trouble. Paul is taken to Athens while Silas and Timothy remain behind.

The Holy Spirit was active in Paul's ministry in Philippi, through exorcism and rescue. The Thessalonian and Berean episodes contain no such elements. Certain events, though, remain constant: for example, preaching is always central in forming new Christian churches.

■ **Acts 17:16-34.** Paul is not impressed, seemingly, by the ancient city works in Athens that have come to be known as great artistic and architectural works. The religious idolatry does disturb him. Paul first seeks Jews in the synagogue in order to argue from Scripture against the idols "as well as in the marketplace day by day."

One of the highlights of the second journey is Paul's speech in the Areopagus. Luke pictures Paul as a great orator addressing the assembled Greeks. Taking his cue from an inscription, Paul begins.

Since the Greeks do not have the Scriptures of Hebrew faith in their tradition, Paul cannot argue primarily from scriptural evidence. He begins with what his listeners are familiar with, namely nature and creation. The God who created the world cannot be contained in hand-built buildings. God gives breath and life to all living things. God's creation of all humankind has within it the implicit responsibility of all men and women to seek God. And God is not far away from us. Paul's terms here are not spatial; they are relational. God is close to us in relationships.

In the past our ignorance has been sufficient excuse for not repenting. Now, however, repentance is necessary (verse 30). Paul includes the classic element of summons to repentance to a people quite unfamiliar with the concept. Repentance is related to the inevitable judgment that will be carried out by a man, obviously an allusion to Jesus.

The Athenians scoff at the notion of resurrection. Greek thought, with its Platonic separation of different aspects of life and its stoic aversion to suffering as anything except something to be avoided, simply does not have a place for the Christian doctrine of resurrection. But some of the more thoughtful listeners are intrigued (verse 32).

■ **Acts 18:1-17.** Paul leaves Athens of his own accord, not under order of the authorities or secretly to escape the crowd. He goes to Corinth.

Corinth was an isthmus city with seaports on two sides. It was the capital city of the Roman province of Achaia. Corinth's major function was that of a commercial city, but its reputation was that of utter debauchery due to the temple of Aphrodite and its one thousand temple prostitutes.

An insight into how the missionaries lived from day to day is provided through the relationship of Paul and a Jew named Aquila and his wife Priscilla. All three shared the tent-making trade. Verse 4 gives evidence that Paul had to work during much of the week since he only argued and preached on the sabbath.

Silas and Timothy, not mentioned since 17:15 when they had been left behind in Berea, rather abruptly reappear (verse 5).

Paul's mission always began with Jews. Not until the Jews had refused the salvation of Christ did Paul turn only to Gentiles. Indeed, Paul's soul is tortured by the tragedy of his people's refusal to accept the promise of salvation through the crucified and risen Christ.

■ **Acts 18:18-22.** The rest of the journey is covered in almost breathtaking speed. Priscilla and Aquila accompany Paul on the return journey. In a cryptic reference Luke shows Paul cutting his hair. This reference is to the custom of the Nazirite vow.

They visit Ephesus, and a Christian congregation is bolstered. Presumably Priscilla and Aquila are left there. Could it be that the tent-making trade is more profitable in Ephesus?

Landing at Caesarea, Paul proceeds overland. The journey concludes with Paul's arrival in Syrian Antioch.

DIMENSION THREE: WHAT DOES THE BIBLE MEAN TO ME?

Acts 18:9-10—*The Elijah Syndrome*

Paul's work in Corinth appears to be without grave threat. Luke describes Paul's work as successful. Why then does Paul have a vision? Evidently the work of Christian workers is fraught with the danger of loneliness, anxiety, and the subtle impulse to consider oneself as "me against the world."

Can you think of a time when you were concerned that only you were working for the purposes of God? What made you feel this way? Was it the lack of support from church friends? Did you look for results that were not forthcoming? What made you abandon the notion that only you were working?

Acts 17:2-3—*The Stone of Stumbling*

The notion of a crucified Messiah and the resurrection of the dead are hard to understand for Jew and Greek. The Greeks especially would have had a difficult time understanding the Resurrection.

Greek thought at this time entertained the Platonic notion of a separate existence for both body and spirit. Life itself is transitory and something to be "lived through." But as to suffering having any validity as a means of grace? No such notion could have been envisioned by any Greek thinker.

Except for our familiarity with the New Testament, the idea of suffering as a means of grace would be equally as hard for us to believe. Do these ideas call for meeting the challenge of the cross? Where in "popular" preaching is the summons to suffering as a means of knowing the sufficient grace of God?

Paul speaks of the wisdom of God making foolishness of human wisdom. How do you see this enacted today? In what manner is a crucified Messiah and the hope of vindication through resurrection equally as stunning today as it was in the first century?

Acts 16:13-15, 40; 17:34; 18:19-21—The Subtle Work of the Holy Spirit

For many Christians the work of the Holy Spirit is both wonderful and threatening. The wonderful work includes the remarkable, the unusual, the miraculous, and the spectacular. Accounts of exorcisms, speaking in tongues, raisings from the dead, and visions in the night tend to make us think in spectacular terms. But what of the possibility of a more subdued and subtle manifestation of the presence and power of the Holy Spirit? Is such a notion available to us? And what would the implications be?

Luke's account contains small, almost incidental indications of the work of the Spirit. Reread the Scriptures listed above. Where do you see the work of the Spirit in them? Do you see the work of the Spirit in conversion? What about the work of the Spirit in the ongoing life of the church?

Where is the Spirit moving in your church at this moment? Is your church aware of the less unusual and subtle workings of the Spirit?

*In this way the word of the Lord spread widely
and grew in power (19:20).*

THE THIRD MISSIONARY JOURNEY

Acts 18:23–20:38

DIMENSION ONE: WHAT DOES THE BIBLE SAY?

Answer these questions by reading Acts 18:23-28

1. Who comes to Ephesus proclaiming the baptism of John? (18:24-25)

2. Which Christian followers correct his preaching? (18:26)

Answer these questions by reading Acts 19

3. What does Paul ask the Christians in Ephesus when he arrives there? (19:2-3)

4. What happens when the Christians are baptized in the name of the Lord Jesus? (19:5-6)

5. How long does Paul preach in Ephesus? (19:8-10)

6. What sort of powers are accorded to Paul? (19:11-12)

7. At the conclusion of his successful ministry in Ephesus, where does Paul want to go? (19:21)

8. Describe the conflict that develops between Demetrius and Paul. (19:23-27)

9. A riot is narrowly averted due to the city clerk's intervention. What is his argument? (19:40)

Answer these questions by reading Acts 20

10. Why does Paul change his travel plans? (20:2-3)

11. Which people go with Paul on his journey? (20:4)

12. Why does Paul avoid landfall while on the way to Jerusalem? (20:16)

13. According to Paul's farewell in Miletus, what awaits him in Jerusalem? (20:23)

14. What is Paul's attitude toward his life? (20:24)

15. What perils are in the future for the Christian congregations? (20:29-30)

16. To whom does Paul commit the care of each Christian and Christian congregation? (20:32)

17. How does Paul conclude his time with the Christians? (20:36-38)

DIMENSION TWO: WHAT DOES THE BIBLE MEAN?

In this lesson you will begin to study the third and final missionary journey of Paul. In this account Paul assumes nearly heroic stature as he confronts outside threat and oppression as well as the more subtle but deadly internal division of potential heresy. As we see Paul stride victoriously through many different cities, we will also see danger cast its shadow across Paul's path.

■ **Acts 18:23-28.** Paul's journey begins with visits to churches in the Galatian and Phrygian regions. Within these churches are different theological orientations. Specifically, in this incident the group surrounding John the Baptist exerts its influence. Apollos, an Alexandrian, preaches the gospel regarding Jesus but with one critical element missing. His preaching stops with the baptism of repentance, John's baptism. Presumably he has never heard of the Holy Spirit. Even though Apollos is able to preach effectively, presenting Jesus as the Christ, Priscilla and Aquila must amend his preaching. Paul's association with Priscilla and Aquila began at Corinth. Paul calls them "my co-workers in Christ Jesus" (Romans 16:3). Priscilla and Aquila dedicated their talents and resources to the advancement of the gospel.

■ **Acts 19:1-7.** The incomplete gospel of the Baptist's group is not restricted to one preacher or one place. Now Paul himself must confront the group in Ephesus. Unlike previous events, Paul does not first go to the Jewish synagogue in order to refute the Jews. He goes directly to the Christian disciples.

Paul seems to doubt the genuineness of the disciples' Christianity. He asks about the distinctively Christian element of the Holy Spirit. When the disciples hear of the added dimension of the Holy Spirit, they are baptized in the name of the Lord Jesus. This should not be interpreted as rebaptism. Luke makes a clear distinction between a baptism of repentance and the Christian baptism in the name of Jesus. As the baptism occurs, the Holy Spirit comes upon the assembly.

■ **Acts 19:8-20.** Paul begins the final missionary effort in which he will be free to exercise his full effort and gifts without interference. Once again, he begins with a direct approach to the Jews through the synagogue (verse 8). Two responses develop to the preached word. Some "became obstinate; they refused to believe." Others are intrigued and attracted to the Christian gospel. They leave the synagogue and go to what may have been a lecture hall to hear further Christian interpretation of the Scriptures. Paul continues this ministry for two years. But the influence of Paul's preaching is not restricted to Ephesus alone. The word spreads throughout the entire region, among Jews and Greeks.

In addition to the power of Paul's preaching, Luke shows greater power through miracles and exorcisms (verses 11-12). At this point, Paul is at the apex of his missionary career. This image of the triumphant apostle is the one most often recalled in church history.

Power such as that shown by Paul attracts would-be wonderworkers as well as sincere followers. Itinerant exorcists try to use the name of Jesus without understanding the faith necessary or the extent of the power therein. Luke paints a rather comic picture of exorcists having the tables turned on them. First the evil spirit challenges them, "Jesus I know, and Paul I know about, but who are you?" The final scene shows the frustrated exorcists running naked from the embarrassment (verses 13-16). Luke comically draws attention to the overwhelming authority and victory of Christianity over magic.

So powerful is the Christian victory over magic that scrolls on sorcery are burned and sorcerers confess their deeds. Luke includes mention of the raw economic value of the torched materials to show the impact Christianity can have on realms outside purely religious interests, maybe in preparation for the major conflict about to unfold in Ephesus.

■ **Acts 19:21-22.** Further travel plans are made as Paul, for the first time, indicates his final destination is Rome. Note that no mention is made at this time regarding the collection for the church in Jerusalem. As far as this account is concerned, Paul's primary motive for visiting Jerusalem is to celebrate Pentecost.

■ **Acts 19:23-41.** In Ephesus a tense and explosive situation develops. Christian preaching has gone beyond the doctrinal and moral realms into the economic sphere of Roman religious life. The temple of Artemis, one of the seven wonders of the ancient world, spawned an enormous economy of religious idols, statues, and trinkets. Not only is the Ephesian economy threatened, but the entire region's as well.

The artists also are concerned about the impact Christianity might have on the religious cult (verse 27).

Demetrius, a silversmith, stirs up the crowd into an unruly mob bent on doing harm to the accused offenders. For reasons unlisted, Paul is prevented from going to the public theater to defend his friends and the faith. The scene is one of utter chaos.

One man dares take the responsibility of quieting the mob. But when the mob recognizes him as a Jew, the anti-Semitic impulse flares up and the situation turns even uglier, with re-echoed slogans filling the air (verses 34-35).

Finally, the town clerk is able to grasp some control of the situation. Drawing on the townsmen's pride he points out that the city is well-known for its temple. And with such a reputation there is no need for such outbursts of mob frenzy. The charges are without foundation anyway. If there are legitimate charges let them come through the official channels.

Saner heads finally prevail, and no harm comes to the missionaries. Luke skillfully portrays the power and success of the Christian movement not by describing Christian action but rather through the results that develop after Christianity seeps into the lives of disciples and their culture.

■ **Acts 20:1-6.** Paul makes plans to leave Ephesus after a successful stay there. He heads for the region of Macedonia, which includes Philippi, Thessalonica, Berea, and possibly Corinth. Further conspiracy forces a change of plans after only three months (verse 3).

The Passover gives specific timing to an otherwise indefinite time period (verse 6). As with earlier moments in Acts, considerable activity is compressed into a small amount of space making exact passage of time nearly impossible. The amount of time occupied by verses 1-6 may have been as much as a year.

■ **Acts 20:7-12.** Luke continues his picture of Paul's triumphs in the story of the young man Eutychus. During the story the "we" verses do not appear. Instead rather specific detail is used, thus giving the incident the quality of an eyewitness report, which is exactly what the use of "we" had done earlier.

After the miracle of life, the entire congregation celebrates and continues its worship until daybreak. Paul concludes his work here with a blaze of glory.

■ **Acts 20:13-16.** The story continues with a quick retelling of the rest of their journey. Paul himself takes a different route. Perhaps Paul avoided Ephesus because of lack of security.

The reason for the trip to Jerusalem is so that Paul, a man who never forsakes his people (the Jews), can be there for Pentecost. The collection for the relief of Christians in Judea is not mentioned.

■ **Acts 20:17-38.** At Miletus, only a few miles from Ephesus, Paul sends for the elders of the Ephesian church and makes his final address to them.

The first part of the farewell is a backward glance at what has been done, especially in Ephesus. Paul's ministry has been marked by humility, tears, and persecutions. Throughout his work both public and private Paul has always preached the whole counsel of God, including repentance and faith in our Lord Jesus Christ.

Present circumstances take up the second part of the farewell. Paul's travels are "compelled by the Spirit." Thus, Paul cannot change the plans without defying the Spirit. Suffering and death are clearly a real possibility as Paul indicates that he is ready to give his life if necessary on behalf of the gospel (verse 24).

The third part of the farewell looks to the future not only for Paul but for the churches as well. The future for both is shadowed. For Paul the shadow of personal danger sends a chill wind through the soul. For the church the shadow of heresy sends its chill across the landscape. If anyone should stray from the faith it will not be Paul's responsibility. The elders are reminded of their role as shepherds of the flock.

The speech ends with blessings and exhortations (verses 32-34). The elders are admonished not to seek economic gain at the expense of their congregations. Nor are they to live off the wealth of their congregations. Paul's words attributed to Jesus are not found in any of the Gospels. The point Luke makes is that Paul's final words are his Lord's words.

The final departure is one of great sorrow and sensitive caring and relationship. The Christian assembly shares the kiss of peace after which Paul leaves, never to be seen by these Christians again.

DIMENSION THREE: WHAT DOES THE BIBLE MEAN TO ME?

Acts 19:11-19—*The Liability of Secondhand Faith*

In one sense the confrontation between the exorcists and the evil spirit is quite comical. After all, the exorcists run away naked and defeated. The seriousness of the situation, however, is not lost. Whenever persons confront evil they must take with them a faith that is their own. However, the Christian faith is corporate, not simply private, so the wisdom and counsel of trusted faith partners is essential.

Think of a time when you had to confront an evil or a demand for which you did not have an answer. Did you try to say something that you had heard someone else say? How did it go? Did the spoken word prove to be sufficient? Did previous lessons from wise ones in the faith have any bearing or influence?

As you think of the evils or circumstances in your life or the life of your community, what are the issues you wish to confront and challenge? What do you see as someone else's idea of what ought to be done? Can you use that other person's idea? Do you need to develop your own strategy and design in order to be effective?

What are the issues that challenge you today for which you do not have sufficient faith and which threaten to send you running off in defeat? How can you, or do you link into the faith community to meet this insufficiency?

Acts 19:23-41—When Christianity Goes From Preaching to Meddling

Christianity is more than something talked about in Sunday school rooms and in preaching. Sooner or later Christianity demands some kind of change in both attitude and behavior. The economic realm is no exception. The riot in Ephesus is just such an instance.

What issues in American culture today have economic roots? What impact would Christian thinking have on those economic realities? What would the impact be on the defense contracts for which many corporations compete in order to survive? What might Christian thinking suggest to the economic disparities in our cities and towns?

As the divide in ideologies and perceptions of faith grow ever wider in the current US culture, how do you work with or through these disparities when people on various sides all apply their faith, as they understand it, but come out in different places?

Can you think of a time in your life when your Christian convictions made an impact on how you used your family's resources? What was it? How has that change affected your family's life?

You will be his witness to all people
of what you have seen and heard (22:15).

10

THE ARREST OF PAUL

Acts 21:1–22:29

DIMENSION ONE: WHAT DOES THE BIBLE SAY?

Answer these questions by reading Acts 21

1. What do the Christians in Tyre try to tell Paul? (21:4)

2. How is Paul sent off from Tyre? (21:5-6)

3. To whose house do the missionaries go in Caesarea? (21:8)

4. What symbolic act does Agabus perform? (21:11)

5. What is Paul's attitude regarding the prospect of suffering? (21:13-14)

6. Why is Paul cautioned by Christian Jews in Jerusalem? (21:20-22)

7. What advice is given to Paul? (21:23-25)

8. When the Jews do see Paul, what charges are leveled against him? (21:28-29)

9. The Roman authorities seem initially to confuse Paul with whom? (21:38)

Answer these questions by reading Acts 22:1-29

10. In what language does Paul address the mob? (22:2)

11. What biographical information does Paul reveal to the mob? (22:3)

12. As Paul tells of his conversion experience, how does his account differ from the one in Acts 9? Who hears the voice? (22:9; see 9:7)

13. The role of Ananias is increased somewhat in this story. What does Luke show here about Ananias? (22:12-16; see 9:10-17)

14. What triggers renewed anger among the Jews? (22:21-22)

15. How is Paul able to avoid torture? (22:25)

16. According to this account, Roman citizenship could be purchased, as the commander obviously had done. How does Paul say he has Roman citizenship? (22:28)

17. What is the response of the Roman commander when he finds out that Paul is a Roman citizen? (22:29)

18. Complete the following outline of Paul's third journey by reading Acts 18:23–21:17.

Starting in Syria (18:23), Paul travels through _____ and _____ (18:23) to the city of _____ (18:24). The mission in Ephesus continues for more than _____ (19:8, 10). After this successful mission Paul moves through _____ and _____ (20:1-2). After three months he has to move on due to a plot against him. Paul alters his route to pass through Macedonia to _____ (20:5).

The final leg of the journey begins with the farewell at _____ (20:17). In what appears almost an impatient listing of itinerary, Paul completes the journey by traveling through _____, _____, and _____ (21:1). On the trip to Phoenicia the missionaries pass close to _____ (21:3). From there they sail on to _____ (21:3) and land at _____ (21:3).

Against the desire of Christians along his route, Paul continues his journey to Jerusalem through _____ (21:7) and _____ (21:8). The journey ends in _____ (21:15).

DIMENSION TWO:
WHAT DOES THE BIBLE MEAN?

In this lesson you will complete your study of Paul's third missionary journey. After Paul's return from the missionary field he is greeted with enthusiasm and great joy by the Christian assembly in Jerusalem. However, the scene soon turns into one of confrontation and conflict.

■ **Acts 21:1-6.** With the accuracy of an itinerary Luke describes Paul's journey back to Jerusalem. Through Kos, Rhodes, and Patara, with perhaps an additional landing at Myra, the apostle makes his way. At Tyre the cargo vessel on which they have been traveling unloads its cargo. The missionaries take the opportunity to visit with Christians in Tyre for a week.

The Christian disciples at Tyre try to keep Paul from going to Jerusalem. They are concerned about his well-being. This first attempt to sway Paul seems to present a real dilemma. What if the apostle is directed by the same Spirit that seems also to be speaking through these disciples? Could it be the same Spirit? The same conflict will reappear with Agabus.

■ **Acts 21:7-16.** Arriving at Ptolemais (present-day Acre), the missionaries remain for a single day, moving on to Caesarea where they stay in the house church of Philip. There the prophet Agabus performs a symbolic act indicating the dire circumstances that will befall Paul in Jerusalem. Again, one authority seems to be in conflict with another. Both Paul and the prophet are being led by the Spirit. The Christians here also try to prevent Paul from continuing his journey.

Paul decides the issue by stating absolutely that the will of the Lord shall be done. Does this mean to suggest that the will of the Lord is always for the more arduous path? Do the Christians still have to learn that the will of God will by its very nature involve suffering and persecution?

The issue is resolved, at least in Paul's mind. Thus the journey continues to Jerusalem.

■ **Acts 21:17-26.** The initial response to Paul in Jerusalem is one of great joy and enthusiasm. As he had done at the conclusion of the second missionary journey, Paul reports the results of the enterprise to the Christian congregation. James plays a much lesser part than he had during the Council at Jerusalem. Perhaps Luke is indicating a power change in the intervening years.

What follows sounds very much like a sigh of relief and a whistling in the dark. Against the greatness of Paul's successes, the tension of current events stands starkly. Many Jews, and presumably Christian Jews as well, are in an uproar. Common understanding, ignorant though it may be, holds that Paul is a complete apostate. Contrary to the facts of Paul's ministry, he is suspected of speaking against the entire tradition of Moses (verse 21).

A conciliatory action is suggested. In order to show that Paul continues in the Jewish tradition, he is to take a temporary vow.

The compromise restrictions passed by the Council at Jerusalem are listed in verse 25 in a tone that suggests Paul has never seen them before. Some scholars raise issue with this verse since it could be left out without affecting the flow of the story.

Paul heeds the counsel of the elders. He does go with the four men into the temple (verse 26).

■ **Acts 21:27-36.** As the seven-day period comes to a conclusion "some Jews from the province of Asia" see Paul in the temple. Presumably Paul had not been recognized in the interim. Now, however, the accusations and threats begin.

In addition to the charge of apostasy, Paul is also accused of desecrating the temple by bringing a Greek into the hallowed place. Evidence about Trophimus differs. Second Timothy 4:20 states that he had to be left ill at Miletus. We do not know what really happened.

Using an overstatement (verse 30), Luke shows how explosive the tensions are. Paul is seized, beaten, and dragged out of the temple. The riot arouses the Roman garrison. Luke uses the Roman protection of Paul to indicate the Romans' nonaggressive if not sympathetic view of the Christian movement.

The mob scene is one of absolute chaos. No one can make any sense of what is going on. The situation is so bad that Paul has to be bodily carried away by the Roman soldiers in order to avoid a lynching.

■ **Acts 21:37-40.** Using sophisticated language Paul addresses the tribune. Evidently the Roman garrison had acted on the basis of a misunderstanding of exactly who Paul is. During this time extreme nationalists, terrorists called assassins, had been fighting Roman authority. Small wonder the garrison turns out in force at the sound of a riot. Note that Paul does not use the past tense with respect to his identity. He is a Jew (verse 39).

Paul quiets the mob by using the Hebrew, probably Aramaic, language.

■ **Acts 22:1-21.** Paul uses the familiar terms *brothers* and *fathers* to indicate his affinity with Jews. Again he identifies himself as a Jew. Not only had he been born a Jew, he had been trained at the feet of no less a rabbi than Gamaliel.

Paul then tells of his conversion on the road to Damascus followed by the remarkable and quite unexpected direction in which his life then went. For the most part this account is the same as that of Acts 9, with one exception: In Acts 9:7, Paul's companions heard the voice. In this account, his companions saw the light but did not hear any voice (verse 9).

Paul reminds his hearers of his relationship with Judaism by illustrating the devout character of Ananias. The use of traditional Jewish terms ("The God of our ancestors," "the Righteous One") is clearly an attempt to show the continuity of Christianity and Judaism.

The direction of the missionary work has not been the design of Paul. In a vision Jesus himself had directed the work. By Paul's own admission no one would listen to him since he had been a part of the brutal persecution and murder of followers of the Christian Way. The Gentile mission has all along been the will of God (verse 21).

■ **Acts 22:22-29.** At the mention of *Gentiles*, the crowd erupts into chaos again. Shouts demanding Paul's death fill the air. Demonstrations break out.

The situation is so near explosion that the tribune grabs hold of events as best as he can. Paul is quickly taken into the barracks. The tribune, confused by the uproar and obviously uncertain as to what is at stake, intends to torture Paul in order to find out exactly what is going on. At the last possible moment Paul asks the centurion about the law regarding the torture of Roman citizens.

Roman citizenship was possible in two ways. First individuals could purchase citizenship, as the soldier had. Second, people were born citizens, as is the case with Paul.

The scene comes to a close with the Roman soldiers terrified at what they nearly did; for it would have been criminal to torture Paul, a Roman citizen.

DIMENSION THREE: WHAT DOES THE BIBLE MEAN TO ME?

Acts 21:27-39—An Exercise in Historical Imagination

We often read the Bible for what it means to teach or for doctrinal understanding. At least part of the reason for the reading ought to be for the sheer dramatic events contained in Scripture. The arrest of Paul affords an excellent opportunity to exercise our imagination.

Reread the account. What are the sights and sounds of the event? What does the scene look like? What emotions run high and nearly at fever pitch? What do the faces of the people in the mob look like? What do the soldiers look like?

Acts 22:1-21—An Unresolved Question

The impression left at the conclusion of the Council at Jerusalem is that the Gentile mission is an established fact. However, the rumor of violence and the actual outbreak of mob violence show all too clearly that the issues are a long way from being resolved. Luke uses the incident in order to address his readers as well, so the problem is not restricted to a few Jews in Jerusalem.

Examine your church and your preferences (prejudices?). Are there expectations with regard to social status, or economic level, for membership in your church? While these expectations may not be written down—no doubt they are not—still the expectation may be quite real. To what extent does your church show that the problem of certain types of people being unwanted in the church still exists?

Acts 22:17-21—Personal Preference or Jesus' Prerogative?

Paul's work took a different tack than the one he had intended. The persecutor became one of the persecuted, the former antagonist became a champion for the cause. Does Jesus' will for his church still prevail in people's lives? What are some ministries to which you believe Jesus calls his church? To what extent are those ministries avoided because of personal preference? What are some of the efforts to which you felt called but wanted to avoid?

*Paul looked straight at the Sanhedrin and said,
"My brothers, I have fulfilled my duty to God in all good
conscience to this day" (23:1).*

11

PAUL ON TRIAL

Acts 22:30–24:27

DIMENSION ONE:
WHAT DOES THE BIBLE SAY?

Answer these questions by reading Acts 22:30–23:35

1. Why is Paul brought before the Jewish authorities?
(22:30)

2. What happens to Paul after he declares his clear
conscience? (23:2)

3. Does Paul recognize the high priest? (23:5)

4. Which theological supposition does Paul center on when
talking with the Sanhedrin? (23:6-8)

5. Why do the Roman authorities become involved? (23:10)

6. How is Paul encouraged during his first night in the Roman jail? (23:11)

7. Who conspires to kill Paul? (23:12-15)

8. Describe the precautions taken by the Roman authorities to protect Paul. (23:23-24)

9. According to the letter sent to Felix, what are the charges against Paul? (23:26-30)

10. Where is Paul kept while in Caesarea? (23:35)

Answer these questions by reading Acts 24

11. Who speaks for the delegation from Jerusalem? (24:1-2)

12. What is the first charge brought against Paul? (24:5)

13. What is the second reason for Paul's arrest? (24:6)

14. Paul discounts the possibility of spreading rebellion since he has only been in Jerusalem for a short time. How long has he been in Jerusalem? (24:11)

15. Why has Paul come to Jerusalem? (24:11)

16. How does Paul link the Jewish tradition and faith with the Christian faith? (24:14-15)

17. Which of the charges is the real problem according to Paul? (24:21)

18. Why does Felix delay judgment and put Paul in jail? (24:22)

19. What is the real reason for Paul's imprisonment? (24:26)

DIMENSION TWO: WHAT DOES THE BIBLE MEAN?

This lesson studies Paul's trial before the Sanhedrin and before the Roman governor Felix. Scholars have noted how difficult the trial proceedings are to reconstruct. Many details make any historical reconstruction nearly impossible. However, we must recognize that Luke's major purpose was not merely the representation of historical fact. Central in Luke's purpose would have been the issue or issues that occupied the interests and thinking of his contemporary Christian community. Thus, we will see throughout the trial the following issue in many different expressions: Christianity's relationship with Judaism.

■ **Acts 22:30–23:5.** The scene opens on the morning following the riot in the temple. The commander had presumably called an end to the proceedings with the intention of later finding out what had happened.

Occupying center stage in the drama, Paul assumes the initiative by declaring his own clear conscience. The result is that Paul has no fear of what either Roman or Jewish authorities can charge him with.

Offended by the boldness of Paul, the chief priest orders his servants to strike Paul. Paul reacts with a scathing curse that he later modifies because he did not recognize the chief priest at first. Clearly Paul does not want to show himself removed from the respect of traditional Jewish custom.

■ **Acts 23:6-11.** Many interpreters wonder about Paul's clever ruse in verse 6. Some say that the method used by Paul is a devious one. Others point out the genius of Paul's technique in that he divides his opponents. Luke uses the moment to illustrate a link between Judaism and Christianity. Christianity is not a maverick movement breaking away from Judaism. Rather, Christianity is the logical expression of the Pharisaical hope of resurrection.

The commander now assumes leadership (verse 10). Fearing another riot, he ushers Paul away from the hearing. Luke thus subtly shows the tacit affirmation of Roman authority. Clearly Roman authority does not fear Christianity.

At major turning points or incidents of great threat Paul receives a surge of courage through a vision of Christ. In this instance Paul is assured that the mission begun long ago in Judea will continue inevitably to Rome itself.

■ **Acts 23:12-22.** Against the claim of Paul that an essential link exists between Christianity and Judaism, a plot develops against Paul. The Jewish authorities, unable to get a hasty conviction of the apostle, join a plot with disgruntled conspirators.

Paul's nephew, an incidental character in the drama, is introduced with not a single word of explanation as to how he heard of the conspiracy. Luke is not concerned with such details.

Alarmed at the news, the soldiers make arrangements to protect Paul. In the weave of the story Luke indicates the lack of threat felt by Rome with respect to Paul and, therefore, Christianity.

■ **Acts 23:23-30.** Elaborate plans are undertaken in order to protect Paul. A night transport is arranged with a surprisingly large contingent of armed men as guards. Fully two hundred infantry, supported by seventy cavalry along with two hundred spearmen (perhaps bodyguards), are to escort Paul to Caesarea.

A letter explaining the circumstances and charges is to go to the governor Felix. Claudius Lysias can make little more sense of the entire matter than internal squabbles among Jews. Since Paul is a Roman citizen he deserves protection. Therefore, with the threat of conspiracy close at hand, Paul will be sent to a city where passions are not quite so heated and where the accusers can address a higher authority.

■ **Acts 23:31-35.** The journey begins at night. The foot soldiers must march the entire distance to Antipatris (some forty miles away) and on the following day make the return march with little or no rest. The balance of the armed force continues the journey on horseback, arriving safely in Caesarea.

According to Roman law, the accused can be tried in one of three places: in the accused's home province, in Paul's instance Cilicia; in the province in which the crime occurred; or in the province in which the accused had been captured. Evidently the governor has decided that the hearing will be held in Caesarea. The accusers will have to make the trip in order to continue the case. Note how cleverly the narrator shows the Roman officials as sympathetic with the plight of the apostle.

■ **Acts 24:1-9.** After a five-day wait, Ananias, some of the elders, and Tertullus arrive in Caesarea. Tertullus, well trained in both Jewish and Roman law, will prosecute Paul's case.

Tertullus begins with effusive flattery of Felix. The claims Tertullus makes are stretched if not altogether untrue (verses 2-4). Exaggerating the amount of disruption caused by Paul, Tertullus claims that Paul is "a troublemaker, stirring up riots among the Jews all over the world." Furthermore, the Christian movement is described as little more than a bothersome sect. The real charge has to do with desecration of the temple. As Tertullus finishes his case other Jews with him echo his sentiments (verse 9).

■ **Acts 24:10-21.** Given leave to speak by the governor, Paul begins his defense. In such a short period of time (only twelve days) Paul could hardly have caused a serious threat to Roman authority in Jerusalem (verse 11). Thus Paul effectively sidesteps the potential charge of sedition. Then Paul centers on what would be minimally disturbing to Roman authority, the charges of violating Jewish law.

Paul describes himself as a pious Jew performing those tasks that any good Jew would perform. Moreover, he is not a radical maverick breaking away from Judaism. Indeed, the hope of resurrection, which is central in the Christian gospel, is also shared by Jews. Clearly Luke is using this speech to describe the link between Christianity and Judaism for his readers as well. The real difficulty, according to Paul, is not sedition against Rome but rather theological differences with Jews who do not hold to the doctrine of the resurrection.

■ **Acts 24:22-23.** Felix delays a verdict on the pretext of needing the commander Lysias present. Note how Roman authority continues protecting Paul and even extending a certain freedom to him.

■ **Acts 24:24-27.** Roman law notwithstanding, the governor and his wife try to extort from Paul a bribe. But Paul, having offended the governor with the Christian demand for upright moral living, is kept in prison for another two years.

DIMENSION THREE: WHAT DOES THE BIBLE MEAN TO ME?

Acts 24:1-21—An Exercise in Historical Imagination
Before the Bible was read in printed form, it was heard in oral form. Christian congregations would gather and

hear the readings from Old Testament Scripture and from letters and other writings that began to circulate (which would later be included in the canon of what we call the New Testament). In order to appreciate the skill of Luke as a narrator, work with the trial of Paul using the following questions:

What does the scene look like?
Who are the antagonists?
How do the antagonists look at each other?
What tones of voice do you hear?
What sorts of gestures are made?

When you have set the scene for the trial, then you are ready to continue with the discussion questions.

Acts 24:10-21—What Holds Us Together?

For a number of Christians, relationships with Jews are extremely difficult because the Christian demand that Jews (and others) say a specific assent about Jesus ends further relationship. From the Christian perspective, of course, something has to be said to the claims of God through Christ. However, to stress only an acknowledgment regarding Jesus is to run the risk of missing other important ways in which Christians and Jews are indeed related to each other in faith.

Discuss with class members those elements of faith and hope that Christians share with Jews. You might list on the chalkboard or a large piece of paper your observations. What of the common Scriptures (our Old Testament)? What of the common call of God to be a people proclaiming light to others? Do we share with Jews a common hope for the purposes of God being fulfilled? Do we believe in the purposes of God being worked out through history? What do we make of a God who remains faithful to the creation even though creation turns against God? Do we not share a common hope of forgiveness?

Acts 23:1-11—The Authority of a Higher Calling

Luke's picture of Paul in the midst of hostile witnesses and glittering Roman authority is one of great courage. How could Paul maintain such courage? How could Paul keep his head when all around him swirled conspiracy and confrontation?

The story shows Paul encouraged by the words of Jesus. In the midst of it all, Jesus remains with Paul in order to continue the purposes of God.

Can you recall a moment or moments when you too felt surrounded by hostility or a swirl of events that threatened to make you lose courage? What were those circumstances? What gave you strength to maintain your Christian hope and character?

*And now it is because of my hope in what God has promised
our ancestors that I am on trial today (26:6).*

PAUL'S DEFENSE

Acts 25–26

DIMENSION ONE:
WHAT DOES THE BIBLE SAY?

Answer these questions by reading Acts 25

1. Which Roman official arrives in his new province? (25:1)

2. Which people bring charges against Paul? (25:2)

3. Paul defends himself on which three grounds? (25:8)

4. According to this account, why does Paul appeal to
   Caesar? (25:10-11)

5. Who arrives in Caesarea to greet Festus? (25:13)

6. According to Roman thinking, what seems to be the problem between Paul and the Jews? (25:18-21)

7. Why is Paul brought before Agrippa? (25:22, 24-27)

Answer these questions by reading Acts 26

8. Based on Paul's introductory remarks what is Agrippa's religious tradition? (26:2-3)

9. According to Paul, what is the great hope promised to the ancient patriarchs? (26:6-8)

10. How severely had Paul persecuted the followers of the Christian Way? (26:9-11)

11. Describe the events on the road to Damascus according to this account. (26:13-18)

12. According to Paul's defense, why are the Jews now prosecuting him? (26:19-21)

13. According to Paul's interpretation of Scripture, what must happen to the Messiah? (26:22-23)

14. What is Festus's initial response to Paul's defense? (26:24)

15. What seems to be Paul's greatest wish? (26:29)

16. What is the Roman opinion at the conclusion of Paul's defense? (26:30-32)

DIMENSION TWO: WHAT DOES THE BIBLE MEAN?

Our lesson focuses on the rest of Paul's trial. After a period of two years the governorship changes hands. Porcius Festus has succeeded Felix. Luke begins the story with Festus's arrival in his new province.

■ **Acts 25:1-12.** After a short introductory period, the new governor goes to visit another area of his region. Note the classic usage of going "up" to indicate a journey to the Holy City (verse 1).

As if time itself has stood still, the Jewish authorities are ready for the new governor with the old charges. The plot, which had lain dormant for the past two years, is now revived. Do the Jewish leaders expect more Roman foot-dragging? Do the Jews want to do away hastily with the troublesome Paul before the Roman authority has an opportunity to find out exactly what has happened?

Again the Roman authority refuses to play to the hand of the conspirators, and Paul is protected from death by ambush. After a few days, Festus returns to Caesarea. Paul's accusers again must make the journey in order to press their case.

As Paul lists the charges against him a new one appears (verse 8). Paul defends himself against the charges of violating Jewish law and profaning the temple. He also defends himself against a charge of offense against Caesar. Perhaps the Jews brought another charge to show that Paul is a threat to Rome.

Since the problem is in internal one—among Jews and not with the Empire—let the issue be decided by Roman authority, Paul says, and appeals to Caesar. In making the appeal to Caesar, Paul thus assures a journey to Rome.

■ **Acts 25:13-27.** At no point does any Roman official condemn Paul. Here Festus talks with his superior, Agrippa. By Festus's reckoning the reason for the wrath of the Jews is little more than a squabble over *superstition*. According to Roman law, no one can be turned over for summary execution.

Ignorant of the issues over which Paul and the Jews continue to argue, Festus asks Agrippa to arbitrate the hearing (verses 20-21, 26). Agrippa is interested. Christian preaching has attracted more than a mild interest even in the highest places.

With an economy of words the narrator then pictures a scene of Roman imperial glitter and pomp for the entrance of the king and his sister, Bernice. Into the middle of the imperial trappings of obvious authority and might comes the apostle Paul. Even with all the exhibition of spectacle, still the center of attention is the courageous apostle with his sure message (verse 23).

The charges against Paul are briefly told. But the number of Jews against Paul is now exaggerated into "the whole Jewish community." Still, the Romans cannot condemn the man. In fact, no specific charges can be brought from the indictments. Perhaps the highest official in the area can help remedy the impasse. Roman law continues to protect Paul.

■ **Acts 26:1-23.** Agrippa gives permission to Paul to speak. The narrator pictures Paul taking a stance of great authority from which he begins another defense of himself and of Christianity as a whole.

Paul acknowledges the accusations of the Jews. But he will never answer the charges directly. Agrippa, who has a Jewish background, will understand more of the controversy than Festus has.

Paul's defense begins with his Jewish identity. He emphasizes his Jewishness by mentioning Jerusalem. Not only did Paul grow up within the Jewish tradition, but he is a member of the strict Pharisee party. Paul links the Christian hope with the long-held hope of the Pharisees: the resurrection of the dead (verses 6-8). Luke's intention in the second half of the Book of Acts is to show the undeniable link between the Christian movement and its Jewish roots. The hope of the Resurrection has its roots in the promises to the ancient patriarchs.

Paul's defense now centers on a confession that he too acted ignorantly earlier when he too persecuted followers of Jesus of Nazareth. Paul's oppression of the Christians knew no bounds. He had hounded believers in the synagogues, in homes, and even to the far cities.

For the third time in Acts the dramatic conversion of Paul is narrated (see 9:1-9; 22:6-11). The slight changes that occur in the description should not be viewed as inconsistencies. Luke has emphasized the importance of the event by repeating it three times. But to simply restate in exactly the same words would be to bore the reader and listener. Therefore, slight changes are made. Here Paul's authority comes from the high priests (plural). Here all the company traveling toward Damascus fall to the ground.

The foretelling of what Paul will have to endure comes directly from Christ in this account. Earlier the words came from Ananias (9:15-16).

Again Paul and the narrator show that the movement of the Christian gospel to the Gentiles is God's own intention. Surely the Jewish Agrippa would understand that one could not withstand the divine imperative.

Paul states the reason for the present hearing: his preaching to Gentiles has stirred the wrath of the Jews who now want to eliminate him altogether. But Paul says that he has done nothing to violate the traditions of the Jews nor the law of Moses (verses 20-22). The radical element in the Christian interpretation of the Messiah is that the Messiah must suffer and die after which he will be raised from the dead. Isaiah 53 is interpreted by Jews to mean "Servant of the Lord." The Christian interpretation of that same chapter and those same images is that of the "Suffering Servant." The suffering Messiah is still the stone of stumbling.

■ **Acts 26:24-32.** Festus interrupts Paul's defense (verse 24). The narrator thus draws even more attention to the notion of resurrection. Festus's interruption serves to underline the importance of the doctrine of resurrection in the Christian faith. As for Festus, he thinks Paul has read one too many theological treatises or argued one too many times with intellectuals.

Luke's purpose of showing Christianity to be a noble movement and not one bent on revolution or creating civil strife finds expression in Paul's continued defense. Christianity is not a secret society hidden from the balance of society. Indeed, Christianity has been spread in the open, quite publicly (verse 26).

Paul's appeal does not convert the king. But for the moment the Roman king shows remarkable interest in the Christian faith. Luke could hardly have shown lenient Roman authority any more clearly.

In what appears almost an invitation to the reader and listener, Paul says that he wishes all could be like him with the exception, of course, of his chains and imprisonment. Thus, the reader is drawn into the dramatic action of the story.

The story ends with the king and his sister (Bernice) rising to leave the proceedings. Once again Roman authority can find no reason for continuing Paul's trial. Had Paul not made the appeal to Caesar, he would have been set free (verse 32).

DIMENSION THREE: WHAT DOES THE BIBLE MEAN TO ME?

Acts 26:16—Appointed to Serve

God still summons persons to the task of proclaiming the claim of God on all life. For this task, God needs people. The message in broad strokes has to do with God's intention for the entire creation. As with biblical folk so with moderns who hear such a summons.

What kind of God is this who requires men and women to speak? Have you ever felt the urge to proclaim the claim of God through Christ? Do you know anyone who has felt the summons of God to a specific task?

What are some issues to which God would have men and women speak today? Are social issues such as poverty, racism, armament build-up, and economic disparity parts of life to which God has a word to speak? What are some specific areas of our lives to which the summons to repentance needs to be proclaimed loud and clear?

Acts 26:19-28—The Plight of Theology in a Cynical World

Many people who hear the Christian message scoff at the prospect of such peculiar perspectives and insight in the rough-and-tumble world of reality. Yet, throughout history the Christian gospel has survived and emerged from every age of doubt and cynicism as the still-hopeful word of life.

Luke's account of Paul amid Roman splendor illustrates one way in which the Christian can live in the real world. The firm resolve of the apostle with his message of hope stirs both cynicism and wonderment. What more can we hope for as we proclaim our gospel?

Are we satisfied with the opportunity to present our message? Or are we insistent on its approval and acceptance by people as well?

What do you think are the possibilities for proclamation in a world like ours? Where do you see hopeful signs that the gospel is faithfully being proclaimed?

Acts 26:23—The Gospel of Resurrection

The Roman response to the doctrine of resurrection is one of incredulity if not outright cynicism. For the Roman mentality, death is the end of everything. The moment of death is the moment at which all the hopes, dreams, and intentions of a person come to an absolute end.

From the Christian point of view, of course, resurrection implies the continuation of the drama of God's will. The individual himself or herself may pass from the scene but the will of God cannot be so arbitrarily ended.

Reflect on the hope of resurrection. What difference does having a resurrection hope make for people these days?

We boarded a ship . . . and we put out to sea (27:2).

13

PAUL'S JOURNEY TO ROME

Acts 27–28

DIMENSION ONE: WHAT DOES THE BIBLE SAY?

Answer these questions by reading Acts 27

1. Who is responsible for Paul's travel to Rome? (27:1)

2. In addition to Paul and the narrator, who goes with the company? (27:2)

3. What does Paul predict about the rest of the journey from Fair Havens? (27:8-10)

4. What is the hope Paul offers to the ship and its crew? What gives him that hope? (27:22-25)

5. How long does the vessel drift in the Adriatic (Sea of Adria)? (27:27)

6. How are Paul and other prisoners saved from death? (27:42-43)

Answer these questions by reading Acts 28

7. Where does the ship's company land? (28:1)

8. How do the islanders show kindness toward the shipwrecked company? (28:2)

9. What happens to Paul? (28:3-6)

10. Whom does Paul heal? (28:7-8)

11. Whom does Paul first look for in Rome? (28:17)

12. According to this account, why did Paul make his appeal to Caesar? (28:19)

13. How long does Paul continue to preach the gospel in Rome? (28:30)

14. Complete the following outline of Paul's journey to Rome.

Paul and other prisoners are turned over to the centurion _____ (27:1). Intending to sail along the coast of Asia Minor, the ship sails to _____ (27:3). Next the ship sails on the lee side of _____ (27:4), arriving at _____ (27:5). Boarding a different ship, the company continues with some difficulty to _____ (27:7) and then under the lee of _____ (27:7), near the port of _____ (27:7). They sail along the coast to _____, near the city of _____ (27:8).

Midwinter voyages are perilous affairs at best. Paul predicts a terrible outcome. Nonetheless, the voyage continues toward _____, a Cretan harbor (27:12). A storm forces the voyage off course. Sailing to the south of _____ (27:16), the ship's crew desperately tries to avoid the shoals of Syrtis. As the storm increases in its ferocity the ship is driven for two weeks across the _____ (27:27). Landfall is finally made on the island of _____ (28:1).

Three months later, after Paul's miraculous survival of being bitten by a poisonous snake (28:3-6) and healing of Publius's father (28:7-8), the journey continues. The first port of call is _____ (28:12) where the travelers stay for three days. From there the company continues to _____ (28:13) and _____ (28:13). Along the way the travelers stop at two well-known resting areas: _____ and _____ (28:15). Finally Paul arrives in Rome.

DIMENSION TWO: WHAT DOES THE BIBLE MEAN?

■ **Acts 27:1-12.** Acts 27 begins with one of the best sea-voyage stories from all antiquity. This story is one of the longest in the entire Bible covering many episodes and quite a long distance. Paul will be transported to Rome as a prisoner. However, some of his friends will accompany him. The dangerous voyage will begin with passage along the coast of Asia Minor.

Throughout the second half of Acts the narrator has in many instances shown how Romans at every level treat Paul kindly. At Sidon, Julius allows Paul time to visit with his Christian friends (verse 3).

The journey continues with a change of ships at Myra in Lycia. It seems the centurion has the authority to secure passage on cargo vessels for prisoners of the empire.

The ship makes headway but only slowly, as the prevailing winds prevent rapid passage. Finally, the vessel comes to the harbor called Fair Havens (verse 8). Though the story has taken only eight verses to tell, a great deal of time has elapsed since the party set sail from Caesarea. Luke's telescoped account in Acts makes it difficult to get a sense of time and distance.

Already the ship is behind schedule; critical time has been lost. Now the journey will last into the perilous midwinter time when sea travel is all but impossible. Paul predicts a terrible fate for the ship and all hands on board (verse 10).

The centurion assumes more authority than in fact he would have had. Listening to the captain and the owner he decides to continue the journey. Wintering in Fair Havens is impossible. Another harbor must be found.

■ **Acts 27:13-26.** Favorable winds begin to blow. But soon after the ship begins the voyage, the dreaded northeast winds strike and a terrible storm erupts on the sea. The bulky, hard-to-handle ship cannot turn into the wind. Therefore, the ship can only turn stern to the wind and run with it.

Raging seas threaten to break the ship apart. In a relative calm the crew try to secure the ship and check out the lifeboat to make certain it will be serviceable in event of shipwreck.

The storm whips up again forcing not only reefing in the sails, but jettisoning material (throwing cargo overboard) (verse 18). Clearly the ship and its company are in peril of shipwreck. Luke pictures the ship storm-tossed and nearly breaking apart, sailors and soldiers alike nearly panicking at the prospect of death. To make matters worse the wind-driven clouds make any bearings impossible. Luke paints a picture of utter disaster.

In the midst of a terrible storm and tossing seas Paul assumes the stance of an orator. Anyone who has ever been on the ocean in even a moderately tossing sea must be amused at the sight. Hardened veterans of the sea, the crew have been unable to eat for days. The entire crew and company wonder how the ship will hold together. Luke clearly uses the occasion, unrealistic but dramatic, to give Paul the opportunity to proclaim hope.

Paul moderates his first prediction (verse 10). The vessel will be lost; but no death will occur. The reason no death will occur is that God intends for Paul to appear in Rome. Therefore, since God will save one, all will be saved (verse 24).

■ **Acts 27:27-32.** For two weeks the vessel is adrift in the Adriatic. At night the sailors take readings. Quickly they read shallower waters. The ship will run aground soon. Midnight darkness and the roar of breakers creates near panic on board. The soldiers and sailors, in sharp contrast to the confident Paul, distrust each other. As the sailors attempt to take an anchor further away from the ship in order to secure it for the rest of the night, the soldiers fear an abandoned ship. The small lifeboat is cut free. Now the large and cumbersome vessel must be beached the next day.

■ **Acts 27:33-38.** These verses seem almost unnecessary to the account of a harrowing night's anxiety in pounding surf. The picture is of the apostle Paul in the midst of life-threatening turmoil taking bread and performing something akin to the sacrament of Communion. For the second time, Paul assures the ship's hands that all will be well. Even in the midst of turmoil the Eucharist (Communion) can be celebrated since God remains faithful to God's promises.

■ **Acts 27:39-44.** The story of shipwreck resumes with the dawn. Casting off the anchors, the crew tries to beach the ship. In the unfamiliar waters the ship runs aground, bow first. Immediately the ship begins to break up.

Showing the care of the centurion even while near panic grips everyone else, Luke tells how the prisoners narrowly escape death. Escape was by far the last possibility for them. Chained prisoners would in all likelihood drown still chained to the ship. Luke thus uses this event to show once again the protection given Paul by the Romans. Grasping splintered planks the entire company is washed ashore (verse 44).

■ **Acts 28:1-10.** Following their close shave, the ship's company learns that they have made landfall on the only island within hundreds of miles, Malta. Thus, the promise of 27:26 is fulfilled.

The islanders offer help to the shipwrecked company, building a fire to warm and dry them. As Paul busies himself helping the shivering survivors, he is bitten on the hand by a viper. Few stories in the Bible cause stranger responses than this one. For some Christians, this story implies that anyone thoroughly committed to the Lord should be able to handle poisonous snakes. Luke's purpose, however, is to show that even in the midst of trial and desperation the apostle remains empowered with miraculous power and is protected by God.

After the story of the poisonous snake is the scene of a miraculous healing (verses 7-9). The account is thus underscored with the power that remains with the apostle. Some interpreters point out the specific medical terms used in this short story as evidence that, indeed, Luke the physician is the writer of Acts.

■ **Acts 28:11-22.** For three months the company winters on Malta before continuing on their journey to Rome. Through

GENESIS to REVELATION **ACTS**

Syracuse, Rhegium, and on to Puteoli, the band of travelers moves, finally arriving in Rome (verse 14b).

They arrive in Rome twice (verses 14 and 16). How can we reconcile what appear to be two different arrival stories? Scholars point out that Luke has been using different sources throughout Acts. Here the problem of combining sources is quite apparent. Perhaps Luke inserts verse 14 in order to allow time to make Paul's arrival in Rome known.

In any event, Paul arrives in Rome. Allowed relative freedom, Paul invites the leaders of the Jews to his quarters. Here in the last scenes of Acts, Luke takes great care to show Paul is still concerned with the relationship between Judaism and Christianity. Paul did not arbitrarily estrange himself from the Jewish roots of tradition and Scripture.

Luke's purpose of showing the lack of threat that Christianity poses to Rome finds similar expression. The Romans at every turn have been unable to find any offense that would warrant prosecution (verses 18-19).

Paul's and, therefore, Luke's interest in the continuity between Judaism and Christianity is once again stated. The relationship has to do with shared theological hopes. Paul's reputation has not preceded him to Rome. However, word about the Christian movement is already there.

■ **Acts 28:23-29.** From his lodging Paul does exactly what he had begun to do so many years earlier. Arguing from Scripture Paul explains the Christian interpretation of the Messiah, the Messiah's suffering, death, and resurrection. As with earlier sermons this moment produces two different responses (verse 24): Some of the people believe and others are left unconvinced.

But even the rejection of the gospel does not confound nor disturb Paul. The Holy Spirit has already indicated this rejection in the prophet Isaiah's work (verses 25-27).

Luke makes a concluding statement about the entire Gentile mission (verse 28). Authorized by the Holy Spirit, the mission to the Gentiles is necessary because the Jews rejected the gospel.

■ **Acts 28:30-31.** The Book of Acts ends with a remarkable irony. On the one hand is the prisoner Paul remaining in captivity for over two years. But on the other is the towering affirmation that external circumstances notwithstanding, the gospel itself is still unchained. The gospel is still preached openly.

DIMENSION THREE: WHAT DOES THE BIBLE MEAN TO ME?

Acts 28:31—A Concluding Hope

The story in Acts comes to a hopeful conclusion. But the story itself continues for thousands of years, up to and including our own time. Luke describes Paul's preaching as open and unhindered.

Christianity began as an obscure movement of a mere handful of people. But by the power of the Spirit the once minimal number has been transformed into a power that the entire world has to come to terms with. Throughout the centuries many people have tried to sound the death knell of the church. Yet the pallbearers have repeatedly had to take off their gloves as the church refuses to die. Surely this historical survival gives us sufficient reason for hope.

But challenges still face the church. Think of issues that you believe challenge the church today. To what extent do these issues restrict the gospel of Christ? To what extent does the gospel refuse to be confined?

If Luke were writing today could he conclude with the same hope he shows at the end of the first century? Where do you see the gospel holding life together?

Acts 28:31—The Struggle for an Unhindered Gospel

Throughout the Book of Acts the narrator takes great pains to show the blatant and subtle ways in which men and women would hinder the spread of the gospel of Christ. Yet, at the end of the story he implies that the gospel continues unchecked.

Today many people are still wondering about the extent of the gospel. Many churches are still socially and economically divided. Racial barriers are still in place, if not officially then emotionally and intellectually, among church members. Differing theological views threaten to make the gospel a splintered entity rather than a universal hope.

Where do you see hope for an open gospel? Where are words of challenge and confrontation needed in order to insure an open gospel? What do you need to say in order to help the gospel reach its universal hope?

Thank God for the work of the gospel begun so long ago yet which remains as lively as today's discussion. Ask for the continued presence of the Holy Spirit in all your individual and corporate lives so that all of every age and station will hear the gospel of Christ.

About the Writer

Dr. James E. Sargent is a former pastor in The United Methodist Church, having served in the West Ohio Conference.

CPSIA information can be obtained
at www.ICGtesting.com
Printed in the USA
LVHW022010280820
664032LV00006B/32